William M. Seavey

The Powers and Duties of Notaries Public

and justices of the peace in Massachusetts

William M. Seavey

The Powers and Duties of Notaries Public
and justices of the peace in Massachusetts

ISBN/EAN: 9783337220686

Printed in Europe, USA, Canada, Australia, Japan

Cover: Foto ©Suzi / pixelio.de

More available books at **www.hansebooks.com**

THE POWERS AND DUTIES

OF

NOTARIES PUBLIC

AND

JUSTICES OF THE PEACE

IN

MASSACHUSETTS.

BY

W. M. SEAVEY,

AUTHOR OF "THE MASSACHUSETTS TOWN OFFICER."

BOSTON:
LITTLE, BROWN, AND COMPANY.
1894.

University Press:
JOHN WILSON AND SON, CAMBRIDGE, U.S.A.

PREFACE.

————◆————

THE author has endeavored in the present work to state in a concise form all the provisions of law which pertain to the powers and duties of notaries public and justices of the peace in this Commonwealth.

The powers of notaries public with respect to the protest of commercial paper are derived principally from the cases decided by the Supreme Judicial Court. These cases have been carefully selected, and to them have been added decisions from some of the important cases on the subject in other jurisdictions, combined with suggestions from the practical experience of notaries public and bank officers in this Commonwealth.

The other powers of notaries public, and those of justices of the peace, are almost wholly statutory. The statutes relating to these subjects have been collected, and to these have been added selections from the latest decided cases of the Supreme Judicial Court, wherever these tended to make the meaning of the statutes clearer, and a selection of appropriate forms.

The Index has been made very full, so that one may readily find the provisions relating to the subjects treated of in the book.

W. M. S.

Boston, December, 1893.

TABLE OF CONTENTS.

PART I.

NOTARIES PUBLIC.

CHAPTER IV.

PART II.

JUSTICES OF THE PEACE.

CHAPTER I.

CHAPTER V.

CHAPTER VI.

CHAPTER VII.

TABLE OF CASES.

PART I.

NOTARIES PUBLIC.

PART I.

NOTARIES PUBLIC.

———◆———

CHAPTER I.

ORIGIN OF THE OFFICE OF NOTARY PUBLIC.

§ 1. The office of notary public is of very ancient origin, and has been known to the majority of the Christian nations for hundreds of years. In those countries which have taken the Roman law as the basis of their legal system, the duties of notaries public are of the greatest importance and very varied in their character, while in countries like the United States and England, which use the common law of England, the duties are much more limited. As notaries public are found in nearly all parts of the civilized world, they were formerly of very great use to shipmasters, merchants, and other persons having dealings with foreign nations, in attesting writings and in certifying to acts done by them or in their presence, which might require to be proved in foreign countries. Now, however, the office is of less importance in its international

1

relations than it was formerly. At the present time states and countries have defined by statutes the majority of the acts which notaries of foreign countries and of places outside of their own jurisdiction, as well as those of their own appointment, may perform, and the effect of these acts and the uses which may be made of notarial certificates within the respective jurisdictions of the states and countries have also been defined by statute.

§ 2. In England notaries public were originally appointed by the authority of the Pope of Rome, but since the passage of the Statute of 25 Hen. VIII., ch. 21, they have been appointed by the Court of Faculties of the Archbishop of Canterbury.

§ 3. In Massachusetts the first mention that is made of the office is under the Charter of the Colony of Massachusetts Bay, where notaries public were elected by the General Court, which prescribed the oath to be taken by them and some of their duties and established their fees and the form of their seals, which were engraved at the expense of the Colony. They were also exempted from militia service.

§ 4. Until the year 1720 notaries public were appointed by the Governor and Council, in the same manner as judicial officers were appointed. But in that year the House of Representatives contended that notaries public should be elected by the General Court, in accordance with the clause in the Charter which granted power to that Court " to

name and settle annually all civil officers" except
those otherwise provided for in the Charter, subject to the approbation of the Governor.   This
claim was conceded, and afterwards notaries public were elected by the Council and House of Representatives in concurrence.

§ 5. No Provincial statute was passed which
defined any of the duties of notaries public, although their fees were established by statute.   The
only duties which they performed under the Prov-
ince Charter were those which were attached to
the office by custom.

§ 6. The Constitution of the Commonwealth as
originally adopted provided that notaries public
should be chosen annually by joint ballot of the
Senators and Representatives in one room; but
this was changed by the Fourth Amendment to
the Constitution, so that now notaries are appointed by the Governor in the same manner as
judicial officers are appointed, and they hold their
offices for seven years.

§ 7. At the present time notaries public in this
Commonwealth are empowered by statutes to perform various acts in addition to the presentment
and protest of foreign bills of exchange and the
noting and extending of marine protests, which are
attached to the office of notary public by custom.[1]

---

[1] Opinion of the Justices, 150 Mass 586.

CHAPTER II.

METHOD OF APPOINTMENT.

§ 8. Notaries public shall be appointed by the Governor in the same manner as judicial officers are appointed, and shall hold their offices during seven years, unless sooner removed by the Governor, with the consent of the Council, upon the address of both houses of the legislature.[1] They shall have jurisdiction and the right to act in any and all of the counties of the Commonwealth. And this provision applies to all notaries public appointed before the passage of this act (March 2, 1891), as well as to those appointed after it.[2]

§ 9. There is no statute prescribing the qualifications which persons must have to be appointed notaries public. The requisites which are established by custom are that the applicant for the office of notary public must be a citizen of the United States, a resident of Massachusetts, more than twenty-one years of age, of high standing and character, and he must not be an officer or em-

---

[1] Mass. Const. Amendments, Art. IV.
[2] Sts. 1891, ch. 38.

ployee of a national bank. A woman is not eligible for the office.[1]

§ 10. A blank application similar to the following form may be obtained at the office of the Secretary of State. As applications for the office of notary public are scrutinized very carefully, the strongest possible reasons should be alleged to show the necessity for the appointment, and the applicant should secure the names of prominent men as signatures to the application, so that, if need be, they could urge the appointment in person.

Form of Application for the Office of Notary Public.

COMMONWEALTH OF MASSACHUSETTS.

To His Excellency the Governor:

We hereby recommend [here state applicant's name in full], of [residence, including street, number, and town or city]. [business address, including street, number, and town or city], for appointment to the office of notary public for the Commonwealth of Massachusetts.

He is a citizen of the United States, a resident of Massachusetts, more than twenty-one years of age, and of high standing and character. He is not an officer or employee of a national bank.

[Strong reasons should be given to show necessity for appointment, — for example, that the applicant has

---

[1] Opinion of the Justices, 150 Mass. 586.

considerable negotiable paper to protest, and that he has occasion to take acknowledgments of conveyances of real estate outside of the State.]

[Signatures of those recommending the applicant.]

.................................., 189 .

§ 11. When the blanks in the application have been suitably filled, it must be deposited in the executive office at the State House. The applicant will be notified in due season, should his application be acted upon favorably.

§ 12. Every person appointed by the Governor to the office of notary public shall be notified by the Secretary of the Commonwealth of his appointment, and if he does not, within three months from the date of such appointment, take and subscribe the oaths required to qualify him to execute the duties of the office to which he has been appointed, his appointment shall be null and void, and the Secretary shall forthwith notify him thereof and request him to return his commission to be cancelled, and shall also certify said facts to the Governor.[1]

§ 13. Every person appointed to the office of notary public shall, before the delivery of his commission, pay to the Secretary of the Commonwealth a fee of five dollars.[2]

---

[1] Pub. Sts. ch. 21, § 4.   [2] Ibid., § 6

§ 14. The following oath shall be taken by every person appointed to the office of notary public, before he shall enter on the duties of his office, to wit: —

"I, A. B., do solemnly swear that I will bear true faith and allegiance to the Commonwealth of Massachusetts, and will support the Constitution thereof. So help me God."

Provided, That when any person shall be of the denomination called Quakers, and shall decline taking said oath, he shall make his affirmation in the foregoing form, omitting the word "swear," and inserting instead thereof the word "affirm," and omitting the words "So help me God," and subjoining instead thereof the words, "This I do under the pains and penalties of perjury."[1]

EXPIRATION OF APPOINTMENT.

§ 15. The Secretary of the Commonwealth shall send by mail to every person commissioned as a notary public a notice of the time of the expiration of his commission, not more than thirty nor less than fourteen days before such expiration.[2]

§ 16. A person who presumes to act as a notary public after the expiration of his commission, and after receiving notice of such expiration, sent as is

---

[1] Mass. Const. Amend., Art. VI.

[2] Pub. Sts. ch. 15, § 14.

stated in the preceding section, shall be punished by fine of not less than one hundred nor more than five hundred dollars.[1]

§ 17. On the death, resignation, or removal from office of a notary public, his records and official papers shall be deposited in the office of the clerk of the courts in the county in which he resided, or, in the county of Suffolk, in the office of the clerk of the Superior Court for Civil Business.[2]

§ 18. A notary public who neglects for three months after his resignation or removal from office so to deposit his records and official papers shall forfeit a sum not exceeding five hundred dollars.[3]

§ 19. If the executor or administrator of a deceased notary public neglects for three months after his acceptance of such office, so to deposit in the clerk's office the records and official papers of the deceased which come into his hands, he shall forfeit a sum not exceeding five hundred dollars.[4]

§ 20. Whoever knowingly destroys, defaces, or conceals the records or official papers of a notary public shall forfeit a sum not exceeding one thousand dollars, and be liable in damages to any party injured thereby.[5]

SEALS.

§ 21. By custom, a notary public must have an official seal, and copies of his records must be

---

[1] Pub. Sts. ch. 205, § 24. [2] Ibid., ch. 18, § 2.
[3] Ibid., § 3. [4] Ibid., § 4. [5] Ibid., § 5.

certified under his seal.[1] The seal used by notaries
public in this Commonwealth consists of a stamp
which makes an impression on the paper which is
to receive the seal, and which contains the name
of the notary and the designation of his office.

§ 22. Judicial notice is taken of the seal of a
notary public as an officer recognized by the commercial world.[2] Therefore the signature of a notary
to an instrument going to a foreign country or to
another state, must be authenticated in some way,
usually in the case of a foreign country by the con-
sul of that country.[3] But in case of a protest made
upon the non-acceptance or non-payment of commercial paper, the notarial seal is sufficient in itself,
without being authenticated.[4]

[1] Opinion of the Justices, 150 Mass. 589.
[2] 1 Greenl. Evid., 15th ed., § 5.
[3] Hutchieson v. Mannington, 6 Ves. 823.
[4] Orr v. Lacy, 4 McLean (U. S.), 243; Pierce v. Indseth, 106
U. S. 546.

CHAPTER III.

THE PROTEST OF COMMERCIAL PAPER.

§ 23. When a bill of exchange is presented for acceptance or for payment, or when a promissory note is presented for payment, and it is dishonored, (i. e. when such acceptance or payment is refused,) a solemn declaration, written by a notary, must be made stating the fact of the non-acceptance or non-payment, the reason for it if any, and that the bill or note is protested. This declaration is known as a protest. Its object is to fix the liability of the indorsers and other parties to the bill.[1]

FOREIGN BILLS.

§ 24. The most important duties by far of notaries public are those which relate to the protest of commercial paper. In the case of the dishonor of foreign bills of exchange, which are bills drawn in one country or state upon a person residing in another country or state, the notarial protest is the sole way in which the dishonor can be proved.

[1] Smith's Mercantile Law, 3d Am. ed., 327.

It cannot be shown by witnesses, or in any other way. And this is true as well when the protest is for non-acceptance as when the instrument is protested for non-payment.[1]

MUST BE FOR NON-ACCEPTANCE AS WELL AS FOR NON-PAYMENT.

§ 25. A holder of a foreign bill of exchange must cause the bill to be protested for non-acceptance if it requires acceptance, and at its maturity he must also cause it to be protested for non-payment by the drawee, and he must give notice of the non-acceptance and non-payment to such antecedent parties to the bill as he intends to resort to for payment. Nor are the duties of the holder varied if the bill be accepted and paid by a friend for the honor of the holder.[2]

§ 26. The custom in Massachusetts is, if a bill of exchange requires acceptance, to cause it to be protested if it is not accepted. Then, if the owner of the bill is near enough so that he may be communicated with before the time for payment of the bill, he is consulted as to whether he wishes the bill to be presented for payment and protested in case of non-payment. If the owner of the bill is so far away that it would be impossible to hear

---

[1] Ocean Bank v. Williams, 102 Mass. 141.

[2] Lenox v. Leverett, 10 Mass. 1.

from him before the maturity of the bill, it is customary to present the bill for payment, and to protest it for non-payment as well as for non-acceptance.

INLAND BILLS AND PROMISSORY NOTES.

§ 27. In the case of inland bills of exchange, which are those in which both the drawer and drawee reside in the same state, checks, and promissory notes, the protest of the notary is an official act, for it is recognized in section 21 of chapter 199 of the Public Statutes, which provides fees for the protesting of bills of exchange, checks, and promissory notes, and by section 22 of chapter 77 of the Public Statutes, which makes protests of these instruments *prima facie* evidence of the fact of dishonor. Thus, although it is not an absolute necessity to have an inland bill of exchange or a promissory note protested in order to charge the indorser, drawer, or maker, still it is not only more convenient in the case of a suit upon the bill or note, but safer, to have all negotiable instruments protested by a notary public, upon their dishonor. A notarial certificate of protest of a domestic bill of exchange or of a promissory note, as well as his certificate of protest of a foreign bill of exchange, shall be *prima facie* evidence of the dishonor, without further proof.[1]

[1] Johnson v. Brown, 154 Mass. 105.

METHOD OF PROTESTING.

§ 28. The usual course is for the holder of the instrument to make presentment and demand for acceptance or for payment, and then, in case of refusal, he must place the paper in the hands of a notary public, who goes and makes presentment and demand again. If payment be refused him, he will then protest the bill or note and give notice to the parties sought to be held.

§ 29. The protest of a negotiable instrument consists of the following steps: first, the presentment of the instrument for acceptance or payment and the demand for acceptance or for payment; second, the noting of the fact of the dishonor; third, the notices to the drawer or to the indorsers of the fact of dishonor; fourth, extending or drawing up the formal protest; and a fifth step might be added, i. e. the recording of the protest.

PRESENTMENT AND DEMAND.

(a.) *When necessary.*

§ 30. A demand and notice is necessary to charge the indorser of a note, although the maker is known to be insolvent.[1] It is also necessary, although a note is overdue when indorsed.[2] Nor

---

[1] Granite Bank *v.* Ayers, 16 Pick. 392.
[2] Colt *v.* Barnard, 18 Pick. 260.

is the infancy of the maker of a note a sufficient
reason for not making a demand upon him for payment. The holder is bound, in spite of the infancy
of the maker, to make a demand upon him for payment, before he can charge the indorser.[1]

§ 31. It is not necessary to make an actual demand upon the maker when a note is payable at a
particular bank, for it is his duty, when the note
becomes due, to go to the bank and make payment.
All parties are presumed to take notice of the
usual hours at which the bank is open. After the
expiration of those hours, the time for payment
has expired, the maker is in default, and the note
is dishonored. But this rule has no application to
a note not payable at a bank by its terms or by
usage, and not placed in any bank for collection.
Therefore a notice to the maker of a note on the
last day of grace to the effect that it is unpaid,
is of no effect to charge the indorser without a
demand on the maker for payment. And this is
so in spite of the fact that the indorser knows that
the maker is insolvent and has absconded.[2]

(b.) *Who may make.*

§ 32. The proper person to make presentment
and demand for acceptance or payment is the
holder of the instrument or his agent, usually a

[1] Wyman *v.* Adams, 12 Cush. 210.
[2] Pierce *v.* Cate, 12 Cush. 190.

notary ; and it is not necessary that the instrument should be indorsed to the notary.

§ 33. A notary public is accredited on account of his known public character, and demand and presentment made by a notary are undoubtedly good and available if he was employed, and if the note was delivered to him, by the lawful holder. The possession of the negotiable bill or note is evidence of the authority under which he acts, and is sufficient without further proof.[1]

§ 34. By the common law and according to the uniform practice in this Commonwealth, the duties of a notary must be performed personally, and not by clerk or deputy. He is a sworn officer, clothed with important public duties, which in their nature imply a personal confidence and trust.[2] Therefore a notary cannot present a bill for acceptance or payment, or a note for payment, by deputy.

(c.) *At what Time to be made.*

§ 35. On bills of exchange payable within the Commonwealth at sight or at a future day certain, and on negotiable promissory notes, orders, and drafts payable within the Commonwealth at a future day certain, if there is not an express stipulation to the contrary, days of grace shall be allowed

---

[1] Shaw, C. J., in Rand v. Hubbard, 4 Met. 252.

[2] Bigelow, J., in Cribbs v. Adams, 13 Gray, 597 ; Ocean Bank v. Williams, 102 Mass. 141.

in like manner as they are allowed by the custom of merchants on foreign bills of exchange payable at the expiration of a certain period after date or sight.[1] But no days of grace shall be allowed on a bill of exchange, note, or draft payable on demand, nor on a check drawn on a bank.[2]

§ 36. The time the instrument becomes due being fixed, the statute gives three days from that time for payment, under the term " grace," unless the contrary be expressly stipulated. Such a stipulation may be in any form of words which convey the idea that it is to be payable without grace.[3]

§ 37. The demand must be made at a reasonable hour on the last day of grace, to be determined by the circumstances of the case. Thus, if the instrument is payable at any place where business was transacted during certain hours of the day, it must be presented during those hours; but if it is not payable at such a place, it may be presented to the maker at his place of residence, and at any reasonable hour.[4]

§ 38. When a draft is payable at sight, it is necessary to present it within a reasonable time after it is received from the indorser. The holder is bound to use reasonable diligence in presenting it, and the question whether a presentment was made within a reasonable time is a mixed question

---

[1] Pub. Sts. ch. 77, § 9.   [2] Ibid., § 10.
[3] Shaw, C. J., in Perkins v. Franklin Bank, 21 Pick. 485.
[4] Farnsworth v. Allen, 4 Gray, 453.

of law and fact, to be decided by the jury under proper instructions from the court.[1]

§ 39. When a promissory note is made payable in a given number of days from the date or from the day of the date, the day of the date is to be excluded in the computation.[2]

§ 40. A demand on the day before the maturity of a note (as before the last day of grace, if the note is entitled to grace) is premature, and will not charge the indorser.[3]

§ 41. A demand made after the maturity of a note is insufficient. Payment should be demanded on the day it becomes due.[4] But where the maker resides at a distant or inaccessible place, a reasonable time will be allowed for the demand to reach him.[5]

§ 42. The holder of a bill payable at a fixed period after date need not present it for acceptance prior to the day of payment. And although it is usual and safe to do so, as he thereby strengthens his security, or, in case of non-acceptance, acquires an immediate right to call on the other parties to the bill, yet he is under no legal obligation to do it.[6]

---

[1] Prescott Bank v. Caverly, 7 Gray, 221.

[2] Henry v. Jones, 8 Mass. 452.

[3] Jones v. Fales, 4 Mass. 245; Henry v. Jones, 8 Mass. 453; Farnum v. Fowle, 12 Mass. 89; Mechanics' Bank v. Merchants' Bank, 6 Met. 13.

[4] Farnum v. Fowle, 12 Mass. 89.

[5] Freeman v. Boynton, 7 Mass. 483.

[6] Fall River Bank v Willard, 5 Met. 220.

But if he does so present it, and it is dishonored and not accepted, he must give due notice of such presentment and refusal to accept.[1]

§ 43. Bills of exchange, drafts, promissory notes, and contracts, due and payable or to be performed on a Sunday, on a Fast or Thanksgiving day appointed or recommended by the Governor of the Commonwealth or by the President of the United States, on Christmas day (when Christmas falls on a Sunday the next day is a holiday), on the twenty-second day of February, on the thirtieth day of May, on the fourth day of July, or on the following day when either of the four days last mentioned occurs on a Sunday, or on the first Monday of September, shall be payable or performable upon the business day next preceding said days; and, in case of non-payment or non-fulfilment, may be noted and protested upon such preceding day; but the holder or holders of such obligations need not give notice of the dishonor, non-payment, or non-fulfilment thereof until the business day next following the days above specified.[2]

§ 44. Upon a promissory note payable on demand, a demand made at or before the expiration of sixty days from the date thereof shall be deemed to be made within a reasonable time ; and any act, neglect, or other thing, which by the rules of law and the custom of merchants is deemed equivalent

---

[1] Rice v. Wesson, 11 Met. 403.
[2] Pub. Sts. ch. 77, § 8 ; Sts. 1882, ch. 49 ; Sts. 1887, ch. 263.

to a presentment and demand on a note payable at a fixed time, or which would dispense with such presentment and demand, shall, if it occurs at or before the expiration of said sixty days, be deemed a dishonor of such note, and shall authorize the holder thereof to give notice of the dishonor to the indorser, as upon a presentment to the promisor and his neglect or refusal to pay the same. A presentment of such note to the promisor and a demand of payment shall not charge the indorser, unless made on or before the last day of said term of sixty days.[1]

§ 45. In order to charge the indorser of a promissory note payable on demand, a demand must be made within a reasonable time, and notice of nonpayment given immediately to the indorser.[2]

§ 46. Orders and drafts for money, payable within the Commonwealth, in which no time of payment is expressed, time notes overdue when indorsed, and promissory notes for a sum certain with interest payable annually but which state no time of payment, are payable on demand, and a demand must therefore be made within a reasonable time upon the drawees or makers in order to charge the drawers or indorsers.[3]

[1] Pub. Sts. ch. 77, § 12.
[2] Field v. Nickerson, 13 Mass. 131 ; Seaver v. Lincoln, 21 Pick 257.
[3] Pub. Sts. ch. 77, § 11 ; Colt v. Barnard, 18 Pick. 260, Converse v. Johnson, 146 Mass. 20.

§ 47. The provisions in the statutes, that, upon a promissory note payable on demand, a demand made at or before the expiration of sixty days from its date shall be deemed to be within a reasonable time and shall authorize the holder to give notice of the dishonor of the note to the indorser, does not apply to such note when it is indorsed after sixty days from its date.[1]

(d) *How and where to be made.*

§ 48. The proper manner of making a presentment of a bill of exchange for acceptance is for the notary to exhibit the bill to the drawee and unequivocally demand acceptance.[2]

§ 49. As a general rule, the person making the demand ought to have the note or bill with him, so as to surrender it if paid. The exceptions to this rule are, where the bill or note is lost, in which case a tender of sufficient security would make the demand valid, without producing the security; and where, from the usual course of business of which both parties are cognizant, the security may be lodged in some bank, whose officers shall demand payment and give notice to the indorser, according to the custom of such banks; the security not being presented at the time of the

---

[1] Rice *v.* Wesson, 11 Met. 400.
[2] Fall River Bank *v.* Willard, 5 Met. 216.

demand, but the parties being presumed to know where it may be found.[1]

§ 50. If the maker has left the state, the holder must demand payment at his actual or last place of abode or of business, within the state.[2]

§ 51. When a resident in the state, after giving a note, removes from the state, and takes up his residence out of the state, it is not necessary to demand payment of the promisor at his new residence, in order to charge an indorser to the note. But where the maker of a note, when it is made and indorsed, has a known residence out of the state, which residence remains unchanged at the maturity of the note, demand must be made on him, or due diligence used for that purpose, and notice of non-payment given to the indorser, before the indorser can be charged.[3]

§ 52. If the maker of a promissory note leaves the Commonwealth, abandoning simultaneously both his residence and his place of business here, although his family remain a few months at the former, it is sufficient to charge one who indorsed the note since the maker absconded, to make a demand at the maker's last place of business, without inquiry at his last residence or of the indorser for the maker's present residence.[4]

---

[1] Freeman *v.* Boynton, 7 Mass. 483.

[2] Wheeler *v.* Field, 6 Met. 290.

[3] Bank of Orleans *v.* Whittemore, 12 Gray, 473.

[4] Grafton Bank *v.* Cox, 13 Gray, 503.

§ 53. When there are several makers of a promissory note who are not partners, the note must be presented for payment to all of the makers, and notice must be given to the indorser of their failure to pay, in order to charge the latter.[1]

ACCEPTANCE.

§ 54. A person upon whom a bill of exchange or draft, which requires acceptance, is drawn, shall have until two o'clock in the afternoon of the business day next succeeding the first presentation thereof in which to decide whether or not he will accept the same; but every bill of exchange or draft which is for cause held over one day shall when accepted date from the day of presentation.[2]

§ 55. The customary method of accepting a bill of exchange is for the drawee to write the word "accepted" across the face of the bill, and to sign his name underneath this; but the acceptance of a bill of exchange need not be by writing upon the bill itself, but a separate written, or even an oral, promise by the drawee to the holder is binding.[3]

§ 56. The drawee of the bill of exchange himself or his agent duly authorized is the only one who can give an acceptance which will be binding. The

---

[1] Union Bank v. Willis, 8 Met. 504; Arnold v. Dresser, 8 Allen, 435.

[2] Pub. Sts. ch. 77, § 17.

[3] Ward v. Allen, 2 Met. 53; Exchange Bank v. Rice, 98 Mass 288; Pierce v. Kittredge, 115 Mass. 374.

acceptance by one partner of a bill drawn upon his firm is sufficient, for in that sense the partner is the agent of the firm.[1]

NOTING.

§ 57. In case acceptance or payment is refused, the notary must "note" the fact on the very day of dishonor.[2] The noting, which may be either upon the protested paper itself or in the records of the notary, is a memorandum of the fact of presentment, of refusal of acceptance or payment, the name of the one to whom it was presented, and the place, the time and date, and signed by the initials of the notary.[3]

NOTICE.

§ 58. When acceptance of a bill or payment of either a bill or note has been refused, the liability of the drawee or indorsee is generally not complete, unless notice of dishonor is sent to him.

(a) Who may give.

§ 59. The notice of demand and non-payment must come from the holder of the instrument, or from his agent, usually a notary. Thus, where a notary sent a notice of dishonor to an indorser, and signed it by mistake with the name of the maker

---

[1] Mason v. Rumsey, 1 Campb. 384.
[2] Thompson on Bills, 315.   [3] Ibid., 312.

as "notary public," instead of signing it with his own name, it was held to be an insufficient notice.[1]

(b) *When necessary.*

§ 60. An indorser of a bill of exchange is entitled to notice of a protest for non-acceptance, although the drawer is insolvent and has absconded.[2]

§ 61. If the drawer of a bill of exchange had no effects in the hands of the drawee, from the time the bill was drawn to the time it became due, he is not entitled to proof of demand and notice of non-payment.[3] Nor is he entitled to notice as indorser where the bill was payable to his own order, and indorsed by him.[4]

§ 62. Where the drawer of a bill of exchange had effects in the hands of the drawee at the time when the bill was drawn, but after the bill was drawn and before it was presented for acceptance the effects in the hands of the drawee were attached, the drawer is still entitled to notice of the non-acceptance, for when the bill was made the drawer had a reasonable expectation that it would be paid.[5]

§ 63. The drawer of a bill on a person who has no funds, but who has agreed to accept and into

---

[1] Cabot Bank *v.* Warner, 10 Allen, 522.

[2] May *v.* Coffin, 4 Mass. 341.

[3] Kinsley *v.* Robinson, 21 Pick. 327.

[4] 1 Met. 109, note.   [5] Stanton *v.* Blossom, 14 Mass. 116.

whose hands funds of the drawer come before
maturity of the bill, is not liable without due
demand and notice.[1]

§ 64. An indorser of a bill of exchange is entitled to seasonable notice of a protest for non-
acceptance, although he indorsed only for the
accommodation of the drawer, and although the
drawer had no effects in the hands of the drawee.[2]

(c) *Form of Notice.*

§ 65. The notice should be such that it will inform the indorser that the note has become due
and been dishonored, and that the holder relies on
the indorser for payment. This information may
be express, or may be inferred by necessary im-
plication from the language used. It is not necessary to inform the indorser of the time, place or
mode of presentment and demand, nor the means
by which it was dishonored, nor matter of excuse
or waiver. Whatever legally fixes the promisor
with dishonor is sufficient, on due notice given, to
charge the indorser.[3]

§ 66. The notice to the indorser must state that
the note has been duly presented to and payment
demanded of the maker, and this is what it means
when the notice states that the instrument has
been " protested for non-payment." And no mis-

---

[1] Grosvenor *v.* Stone, 8 Pick. 79.
[2] Warder *v.* Tucker, 7 Mass. 449.
[3] Gilbert *v.* Dennis, 3 Met. 495.

take or misdescription will render the notice insufficient if it is not of a character to mislead the indorser.[1]

§ 67. A notice by a notary is sufficient if it does not state who holds the note, nor at whose request the notice is given.[2]

§ 68. If the maker of a note has left the Commonwealth before the maturity of the note, the notice to the indorser of non-payment need not state this fact. It is sufficient if the demand for payment has been left at the last and usual place of abode of the maker, or at his place of business.[3]

§ 69. Where a note is payable at a bank, a notice after bank hours, on the last day of grace, that the note "fell due this day, and remains unpaid," sufficiently indicates that the note is dishonored ;[4] and a notice seasonably given to an indorser may be sufficient, although it misstate the day of maturity of the note, and designate the maker by a name not his own, if the indorser is not misled by such errors.[5]

§ 70. A notice to the indorser of a note, which merely states that the note remains unpaid, and that the holders look to him for payment, is not sufficient to charge the indorser, although the

---

[1] Housatonic Bank v. Laflin, 5 Cush. 546.

[2] Shed v. Brett, 1 Pick. 401.

[3] Sanger v. Stimpson, 8 Mass. 260.

[4] Clark v. Eldridge, 13 Met. 96.

[5] Smith v. Whiting, 12 Mass. 6

notice is given by a notary public. The notice must be such as to assert or imply that the note has been presented, and payment refused, or otherwise dishonored.[1]

Form.

B............, ..., 189 .

M..

You are hereby notified that a [bill of exchange, promissory note or check] for dollars $\frac{}{100}$, dated .... , ... , [drawn or indorsed by you], has been [protested or noted] by me for non-[payment or acceptance] after due [presentment and demand] made [upon] the [maker or drawee] this day, and that you are held answerable for the amount, with all legal costs, interests and damages in consequence of the non-[payment or acceptance] thereof.

W. L., *Notary Public.*

(d) *When to be made and given.*

§ 71. To charge an indorser of a note payable on demand, the indorsee must´ give him notice of non-payment upon the first demand on the maker, although such demand was made at an earlier day than was necessary, in order to render the indorser liable on his indorsement, and although the indorsee gives the indorser notice of non-payment upon a second demand on the maker, which would have

---

[1] Pinkham *v.* Macy, 9 Met. 174.

been in season to charge the indorser, if no previous demand had been made.[1] And this applies to a time note indorsed after maturity, as it thus becomes a note on demand.[2]

§ 72. The settled general rule of the mercantile law is that notice to the indorser on the day of the dishonor and after the dishonor, or in the course of the next succeeding day, is seasonable.[3] But notice to the indorser before any demand on the maker is insufficient.[4]

§ 73. If the promisor has absconded before the note is due, without having made provision for its payment, so that no presentment and demand can be made, that is a dishonor, of which the holder may, immediately after the note has become due, notify the indorser ; or if the promisor has agreed that notice left at a particular place shall be deemed a good substitute, and, notwithstanding notice is so left, he does not make payment, this is likewise a dishonor, of which the indorser may be notified at once.[5]

§ 74. The holder of a bill of exchange protested for non-acceptance or non-payment is not obliged to transmit such protest, at the time it is made, to the parties to whom he intends to resort for pay-

---

[1] Rice v. Wesson, 11 Met. 400.
[2] Colt v. Barnard, 18 Pick. 260.
[3] Shaw, C. J. in Grand Bank v. Blanchard, 23 Pick. 307.
[4] Park v. Page, 1 Dane Abr. 425.
[5] Gilbert v. Dennis, 3 Met. 495.

ment; but he must give them seasonable notices of the non-acceptance and non-payment.[1]

(c) *Where and how to be given.*

§ 75. Notice shall be so given, and at such place, that it will be most likely to reach the indorser promptly. Thus, where the indorser was a member of Congress but had his domicile in Boston, it was held that a notice sent to him at Washington, and received there by him, was sufficient to charge him as indorser.[2]

§ 76. When a party to a promissory note, bill of exchange or other negotiable instrument, is entitled to notice of non-acceptance or non-payment of the same, and such instrument is payable or to be accepted, or is legally presented for payment or acceptance, in a city or town in which such party has his residence or place of business, or when for any other reason a notice given to such party in such city or town would be sufficient, such notice may be given by depositing it in a post-office in said city or town, with the postage thereon prepaid, and sufficiently directed to the residence or place of business of the party for the usual course of mails within the limits of said city or town and for the usual course of delivery by postal carriers therein.[3]

[1] Lenox *v.* Leverett, 10 Mass. 1.
[2] Choteau *v.* Webster, 6 Met. 1 ; Young *v.* Durgin, 15 Gray, 264
[3] Pub. Sts. ch. 77, § 16.

§ 77. Prior to the passage of the statute mentioned in the preceding section the holder of a bill or note could not give notice of its dishonor through the mail to an indorser or drawer who lived in the same city or town, but must give the notice to him personally, or at his place of business or residence. The chief object of the statute was to extend the privilege of giving notice by mail to cases where the parties live in the same place.[1] But if it is desirable, the notice may be served by leaving it at the residence or place of business of the indorser or drawer.[2]

§ 78. Under the provisions stated in § 76, *ante*, a notice to an indorser of a promissory note of its non-payment, duly deposited, postage prepaid, in the post-office in the town in which he lives, the direction on the envelope in which it is enclosed containing only his name and that of the town, is sufficient, although he lives on a street which has a name, if the houses on the street are not numbered, and there is no postal delivery by carriers; and the facts that he did not receive the notice, and that another person of the same name lived in the town who did not receive it, are immaterial.[3]

§ 79. Where the notice is served at an indorser's office, it must be served during business hours; but where it is served at his residence, it may be served

---

[1] Wachusett National Bank v. Fairbrother, 148 Mass. 184.

[2] Story, Prom. Notes, § 340.

[3] Morse v. Chamberlin, 144 Mass. 406.

at any reasonable hour before the house is closed for the night.[1]

§ 80. Where the indorser of a promissory note resides in a town where there are two post-offices, of which fact the holder of the note is ignorant, a notice of the dishonor of the note, addressed to the indorser at the town generally, is sufficient, unless he proves that he is accustomed to receive his letters at one of the offices only, and that the holder of the note might have ascertained that fact by reasonable inquiry.[2]

§ 81. A notice sent by mail to an indorser and addressed with the name of the town or city alone, no street and number being used, is sufficient to charge the indorser, if he in fact lives in the town or city named, and unless it appears that there was another person of the same name in the same place.[3]

§ 82. A notice of the non-payment of a note, addressed and sent in due season by mail to an indorser at the post-office where he usually receives his letters, and received by him there on the day after the note fell due, is sufficient to fix his liability thereon, although such post-office is in another part of the same town.[4]

---

[1] 2 Edwards, Notes and Bills, § 829; Bonner v. New Orleans, 2 Woods (U. S.), 135.

[2] Burlingame v. Foster, 128 Mass 125.

[3] True v. Collins, 3 Allen, 438.

[4] Shaylor v. Mix, 4 Allen, 351.

§ 83. An indorser who lives in a town where there is a post-office, is not properly notified of the dishonor of an instrument by a drop-letter left for him in the post-office of another town where the holder resides, and addressed to the indorser as if he also resided there, even though it appears that the indorser is in the habit of resorting to the post-office in each of the two places.[1]

§ 84. Sending notice to the indorser according to an established usage is sufficient, whether the indorser receives it or not.[2] Thus, a notice of the non-payment of a promissory note, addressed to the indorser and deposited in a post-office box in a public street, is sufficient, that being the customary way of sending letters ;[3] and for the same reason notices of non-payment of a promissory note addressed to all the indorsers respectively, and enclosed in a letter to the last indorser, are sufficient to charge the prior indorsers.[4]

§ 85. Where a notary seasonably left a notice of non-payment at a shop near the indorser's place of business, because the indorser was out of town, it was said to be extremely doubtful whether this was sufficient, although the indorser took away the notice the next day or the day after. "Although a man is out of town, yet if he has a domi-

[1] Shelburne Falls Bank r. Townsley, 107 Mass. 444.
[2] Lincoln & Kennebec Bank v. Hammatt, 9 Mass. 159
[3] Johnson v. Brown, 154 Mass. 105.
[4] Wamesit Bank v. Buttrick, 11 Gray, 387.

cile or place of business, it is to be presumed that
he will leave some person charged with the care
of his business, or at least some one between whom
and himself there is a privity or confidence. It is
upon this principle that all notices at one's domicile, and all notices respecting transactions of a
commercial nature at one's place of business, are
deemed in law to be good constructive notice, and
to have the legal effect of actual notice." [1]

§ 86. Where a promissory note specifies no
place of payment, a presentment of it at the
former place of business of the maker, without
any inquiry as to his place of residence, is not a
good presentment to charge an indorser. The
presentment at the former place of business, without any inquiry as to the place of residence, does
not show such diligent search for the maker and
failure to find him as would excuse a want of presentment of the note and demand of payment. [2]

§ 87. Thus it may be seen that " residence " in
the law of negotiable instruments is not used in a
strict sense as necessarily implying a permanent,
exclusive or actual abode in the place, but it may
be satisfied by a temporary, partial or even constructive residence. [3]

[1] Shaw, C. J., in Granite Bank v. Ayers, 16 Pick. 392.
[2] Talbot v. National Bank of the Commonwealth, 129 Mass. 67.
[3] Wachusett National Bank v. Fairbrother, 148 Mass. 185.

(f) *To whom to be given.*

§ 88. The makers and indorsers of a bill of exchange and the indorsers of a promissory note must have notice of protest in order to make them liable, and every person becoming a party to a promissory note payable on time, by a signature in blank on the back of the note, shall be entitled to notice of non-payment the same as an indorser.[1]

§ 89. The several indorsers of promissory notes payable on demand shall, upon due and seasonable notice of the dishonor of such notes, be liable in the same manner and to the same effect as upon the dishonor of promissory notes payable at a fixed time ;[2] and the indorser in blank of a promissory note made payable to his order for value is not liable thereon without proof of notice of its non-payment by the maker.[3]

§ 90. If a bill of exchange is drawn by a partnership, notice to the partnership of the dishonor of the bill is notice to all the members. And if the partnership has been dissolved, and all of the partners have gone away, a notice of the dishonor given at the place where they formerly did business, and received by an agent appointed to wind up the partnership, is sufficient, if the holder did not know of the dissolution.[4]

---

[1] Pub. Sts. ch. 77, § 15. [2] Ibid., § 13.

[3] Webber *v.* Matthews, 101 Mass. 481.

[4] Bliss *v.* Nichols, 12 Allen, 443.

§ 91. Although it is better for the notary to send simultaneous notices of the dishonor of an instrument to all the parties to it whom it is desired to charge, still this is not absolutely necessary, and where there are several successive indorsers of a bill of exchange or promissory note it is competent for the holder to send notice to his immediate indorser, and if each transmits notice after he himself has received it, the indorsers are severally liable, although the notice does not reach the earlier indorsers quite so soon as if it were transmitted to each indorser at once by the party who is holder at the time of dishonor, or by the notary emp'oyed by such party.[1]

DILIGENCE.

§ 92. A notary is required to exercise due diligence in the discharge of his duties as regards commercial paper, but the law does not require of the holder of a negotiable instrument, or of his agent the notary public, the highest and strictest degree of diligence in giving notice of its dishonor, but only such a degree of reasonable diligence as will ordinarily bring notice home to the party; and less diligence is required in ascertaining the residence for the purpose of giving notice than for the purpose of making a demand of payment.[2]

---

[1] Shaw, C. J., in Eagle Bank v. Hathaway, 5 Met. 215.
[2] Wachusett National Bank v. Fairbrother, 148 Mass. 185.

Thus notice of the dishonor of a bill or note is sufficient to charge an indorser or drawer if it is delivered to him personally, or is left at his place of residence or of business, the postage being prepaid.[1] Going to the place of business of the maker of a note, in business hours, with the note, to demand payment of it and finding it shut, without any person to answer inquiries, is using due diligence, and excuses a want of demand, although the note is not expressly payable at such place of business.[2] Where the holder of a bill drawn by a person who had been absent from the state for several years left a notice at his last dwelling-house, none of his family residing there, which came to the hands of the drawer's wife, it was thought that due diligence had been used.[3] But where a note was dated at Boston, where the maker and all the indorsers resided, it was held that the fact that the notary went to various places in Boston, making diligent inquiry of different people for the promisor, but could not find him, nor any one knowing him, nor any one with the funds for the payment of the note, and thereupon sent notices to the several indorsers, did not show reasonable diligence to find the maker which would excuse a want of a presentment and demand;[4] and where the holder of a note of a firm

---

[1] Bank of America v. Shaw, 142 Mass. 290; Importers and Traders' Bank v. Shaw, 144 Mass. 421.

[2] Shed v. Brett, 1 Pick. 413.

[3] Blakely v. Grant, 6 Mass. 386.

[4] Porter v. Judson, 1 Gray, 175.

presented it at the last place of business of the
makers, but which was then occupied by strangers,
and was told that the makers had gone out of the
city without leaving any funds, whereupon he made
no further inquiry for them, but in fact one of them
lived in the city and his name and place of residence were in the directory, it was held that
there had not been sufficient diligence to excuse
a demand.[1]

§ 93. The principle of all the decisions on the
subject is, that reasonable diligence must be used
by the holder in getting notice of the dishonor to
the indorser or drawer.[2]

RECORDS.

§ 94. Notaries public must keep a record in
which their transactions with regard to the protests
of commercial paper shall be set down. These
records must be carefully kept, as they must be
delivered up by the notary on the expiration of
his appointment, under a heavy penalty.[3] A book
prepared for keeping these records may be obtained
from law stationers.

EXTENDING THE PROTEST.

§ 95. While the notary must "note" the fact
of the dishonor of an instrument on the very day

---

[1] Granite Bank v. Ayers, 16 Pick. 392.

[2] Hobbs v. Straine, 149 Mass. 212.

[3] Pub. Sts. ch. 18, §§ 2-4 (§§ 17-19, ante).

upon which it occurs, he may make out the full and complete protest at any reasonable time afterward, before suit is brought on the instrument. The protests must be duly certified by the notary public under his hand and official seal, and shall be *prima facie* evidence of the facts stated in the protest and of the notice given to the drawer or indorser.[1]

Form of Protest of Bill or Check.

COMMONWEALTH OF MASSACHUSETTS.

S.   } ss.

On the   day of   , in the year of our Lord one thousand eight hundred and ninety   , I, A. B., Notary Public, duly admitted and sworn, and practising in said county and [in the city or town of B.], at the request of [the holder] went with the original [bill or check] which is hereto annexed, the time therein limited and grace having fully elapsed, and demanded payment thereof [here state manner of demanding payment]. The [bill or check] remaining unpaid, I duly and officially notified the [drawer and indorsers, — here state manner of sending notice, e. g. by mailing notices properly addressed to them] (postage prepaid) of said [non-payment] requiring payment.

Wherefore I, the said Notary, by request as aforesaid, have protested, and by these presents do solemnly pro-

[1] Pub. Sts. ch. 77, § 22.

test, against the drawer of said [bill of exchange or
check] and all others concerned therein, for
exchange, re-exchange. and all costs, charges,
[SEAL.] damages and interest, suffered and sustained,
or to be suffered and sustained, by reason or
in consequence of the non-payment thereof.

In testimony whereof I have hereunto set my hand
and affixed my notarial seal, the day and year first
above written.

FEES :

  Noting non-acceptance . .
  Postage . . . . . .
  Protesting for non-payment
  Postage . . . . . .

$

A. B., *Notary Public.*

§ 96. Where there have been protests for non-
acceptance and non-payment both, it is only neces-
sory to draw up one formal protest. This may be
done by a form similar to the above, the "Noting
Non-acceptance" sufficiently indicating the protest for non-acceptance. Where protests for non-
acceptance or non-payment alone are required, the
above form may be used by making the requisite
verbal changes.

Form of Protest of a Promissory Note.

[Here affix the original note or a copy.]

COMMONWEALTH OF MASSACHUSETTS.

} ss.

On this   day of   , in the year of our Lord one thousand eight hundred and ninety   , I, A. B., Notary Public by legal authority, commissioned and qualified for said county, and practising in [town or city], at the request of [the holder], of   , went with the original note [if a copy is annexed so state], which is hereto annexed, the time limited therein and grace having elapsed, to [the maker, or place of payment] and demanded payment [here state manner of demanding payment].

The note remaining unpaid, I have officially notified the [e. g. first. second and third] indorsers of the said default by notice addressed to [them], and [here state method of notification].

Wherefore I, the said Notary, at the request aforesaid, have protested, and by these presents do solemnly protest against the maker of said [note], the indorser, and all others whom it doth or may concern, for exchange, re-exchange, and all costs, charges, damages and interest, suffered. sustained and incurred. or to be suffered, sustained and incurred by reason or in consequence of the non-payment of said [note].

[SEAL.]

Thus done and protested in [town or city] aforesaid, and my notarial seal affixed, the day and year last written.

CHARGES:

    Noting,
    Protest,
    Record,
    Notice,
    Postage,

      ———

    $

             A. B., *Notary Public.*

FEES FOR PROTESTING.

§ 97. The fees of notaries public shall be as follows: —

For the protest of a bill of exchange, order, draft or check, for non-acceptance or non-payment, if the amount thereof is five hundred dollars or more, one dollar; if it is less than five hundred dollars, fifty cents; for recording the same, fifty cents; for noting the non-acceptance or non-payment of a bill of exchange, order, draft or check, or the non-payment of a promissory note, seventy-five cents: and for each notice of the non-acceptance or non-payment of a bill, order, draft, check or note given to a party liable for the payment thereof, twenty-five cents: provided, that the whole cost of protest, including necessary notices and the record, when the bill, order, draft, check or note is of the amount of five hundred dollars or upwards, shall not exceed two dollars; and when it is less than five hundred dollars, shall not exceed one dollar and fifty cents; and the whole cost of noting, including recording and notices, shall in no case exceed one dollar and twenty-five cents.[1]

LIABILITY OF NOTARIES.

§ 98. A notary who fails to make a protest when it is required, or who neglects to give proper notice to parties to be charged in case of dishonor, will be liable for the loss occasioned by his neglect; but where due demand upon the promisor has been made by a bank with which a note has been left for collection, a notary by whom the note is protested is not liable for negligence in not making further demand.[2]

RATES OF DAMAGES ON PROTESTED BILLS.

§ 99. When a bill of exchange, drawn or indorsed within the Commonwealth, and payable beyond the limits of the United States, is duly protested for non-acceptance or non-payment, the party liable for the contents of such bill shall, on due notice and demand thereof, pay such contents at the current rate of exchange at the time of the demand, and damages at the rate of five per cent upon such contents, together with interest on the contents, to be computed from the date of the protest; and said amount of contents, damages and

---

[1] Pub. Sts. ch. 199, § 21.
[2] Warren Bank v. Parker, 8 Gray, 221.

interest shall be in full of all damages, charges, and expenses.[1]

§ 100. The rates of damages to be allowed upon bills of exchange duly protested for non-acceptance or non-payment, if drawn or indorsed within the Commonwealth, and payable at a place beyond its limits but within the United States, shall, in addition to the contents of such bill, with interest and costs, be as follows: if payable in the states of Maine, New Hampshire, Vermont, Rhode Island, Connecticut, or New York, two per cent; if in the states of New Jersey, Pennsylvania, Maryland, or Delaware, three per cent; if in the states of Virginia, West Virginia, North Carolina, South Carolina, Georgia, or the District of Columbia, four per cent; and if in any other other of the United States or in the territories thereof, five per cent.[2]

§ 101. The rate of damages upon bills of exchange or orders for the payment of a sum of money not less than one hundred dollars, drawn or indorsed within the Commonwealth, and payable within the Commonwealth at a place not less than seventy-five miles distant from the place where they are drawn or indorsed, when such bills or orders are not duly accepted or paid, shall be one per cent in addition to the contents thereof, and interest on such contents.[3]

---

[1] Pub. Sts. ch. 77, § 18.   [2] Ibid., § 20.   [3] Ibid., § 21.

CHAPTER IV.

POWERS GIVEN BY STATUTE.

ACKNOWLEDGMENTS OF DEEDS.

§ 102. Notaries public may receive acknowledgments of deeds made in this Commonwealth by the grantors, or one of them, or by the attorney executing the deed, and the notary shall indorse a certificate of such acknowledgment upon the deed, or annex the same thereto; [1] and where the acknowledgment of a deed is taken and certified by a notary public, his certificate need not be authenticated by his official seal.[2]

Form of Acknowledgment.

COMMONWEALTH OF MASSACHUSETTS.

S.   ss. ...., 189 .

Then personally appeared the above-named   , and acknowledged the foregoing instrument to be [his] free act and deed, before me.

A. B., *Notary Public.*

---

[1] Pub. Sts. ch. 120, § 6.
[2] Farnum *v.* Buffum, 4 Cush. 260.

§ 103. Notaries public in this Commonwealth may take acknowledgments of deeds conveying real estate situated in the following states and territories: Alabama, Arizona, Arkansas, California, Colorado, Connecticut, Delaware, Florida, Idaho, Illinois, Indiana, Iowa, Kansas, Kentucky, Louisiana (must be certified to before a commissioner of Louisiana), Maine, Maryland, Minnesota, Mississippi, Missouri, Montana, Nebraska, New Hampshire, North Carolina, North Dakota, Ohio, Oklohoma, Rhode Island, South Dakota, Tennessee, Texas, Utah, Vermont, Virginia, Washington, West Virginia, Wisconsin, Wyoming. In the District of Columbia, Michigan, New York, Oregon, Pennsylvania, and South Carolina, the authority of the notary to take acknowledgments must be certified to before a clerk of court, under his seal. It is better in every case to use the notarial seal.

ADMINISTRATION OF AFFIDAVITS.

§ 104. Notaries public shall have the same authority to administer oaths as justices of the peace;[1] and all oaths and affidavits administered or taken by a notary public, duly commissioned and qualified by authority of any other state or government, within the jurisdiction for which he is commissioned, and certified under his official seal, shall be as effectual in this Commonwealth as if administered or taken and certified by a justice of the peace therein.[2]

---

[1] Pub. Sts. ch. 18, § 1.   [2] Ibid., ch. 169, § 74.

FORECLOSURE AFFIDAVITS.

§ 105. The certificate of an entry made for the breach of a condition of a mortgage may be sworn to before a notary public.[1]

OPENING OF SAFETY DEPOSIT VAULTS.

§ 106. A notary public who is not an officer of the company shall, together with the president, treasurer or superintendent of a company organized under the laws of this Commonwealth for the purpose of letting vaults, safes and other receptacles for valuables, be present when such vault or safe is opened because of non-payment of the rent. The notary public shall remove the contents of the receptacle, make a list of the same, and shall seal up such contents in a package, and shall mark thereon the name of the person in whose name such receptacle stood on the books of the corporation, and his address as stated on said books; and such package shall in the presence of the notary and of the president, treasurer or superintendent be placed in one of the storage vaults of the corporation. The notary public shall set forth his proceedings, including the list of contents of the receptacle and his estimate of the total value of the contents, in his own handwriting and under his official seal, in a book kept by the corporation for the purpose.

---

[1] Murphy v. Murphy, 145 Mass. 224.

The notary public shall swear to this statement before a justice of the peace.[1]

PROOFS IN INSOLVENCY.

§ 107. A notary public may take proofs in insolvency. The creditor in person, or if he is unavoidably prevented from being present, his agent, must make an oath before the notary public in substance as follows : —

I,   , do swear that   , of   , by (or against) whom proceedings in insolvency have been instituted, at and before the date of such proceedings was and still is justly and truly indebted to me in the sum of   , for which sum or any part thereof I have not, nor has any other person to my use, to my knowledge or belief, received any security or satisfaction whatever, beyond what has been disposed of agreeably to law. And I do further swear that I have not directly or indirectly made or entered into any bargain, arrangement or agreement, express or implied, to sell, transfer or dispose of my claim, or any part of my claim, against said debtor, nor have directly or indirectly received or taken, or made or entered into any bargain, arrangement or agreement, express or implied, to take or receive directly or indirectly any money, property, or consideration whatsoever to myself, or to any person or persons to my use or benefit, under or with any understanding or agreement, express or implied, whereby my vote for

[1] Sts. 1887, ch. 89.

assignee or my assent to the debtor's discharge is or shall be in any way affected, influenced or controlled, or whereby the proceedings in this case are or shall be affected, influenced or controlled.[1]

SAVINGS BANK AFFIDAVITS.

§ 108. Notaries public may take affidavits under their seals, to be annexed to copies from the records, books and accounts of a savings bank and institution for savings, incorporated under the laws of this Commonwealth, and these shall be competent evidence in all cases equally with their originals. The affidavit must set forth that the affiant is the officer having charge of the original records, books and accounts, and that such copy is true and correct, and is full so far as it relates to the subject matter therein referred to.[2]

[1] Pub. Sts. ch. 157, §§ 29–31.
[2] Sts. 1885, ch. 92.

PART II.

JUSTICES OF THE PEACE.

PART II.

JUSTICES OF THE PEACE.

———•———

CHAPTER I.

ORIGIN AND APPOINTMENT.

ORIGIN.

§ 109. The office of justice of the peace is of very ancient origin. The power of justices of the peace, under the common law, was merely preventive and provisional, except in the case of the smaller class of misdemeanors.

§ 110. In the beginning justices of the peace were merely conservators of the peace, and they had no judicial powers whatever. They were merely officers, with the power to arrest offenders for committing breaches of the peace in their presence. But when Edward III. came into power, judicial authority was given to justices of the peace, and they were appointed by the king.[1] In Massachusetts, justices of the peace originally had the power to try the minor class of causes both civil and

———

[1] 1 Black. Com. 349; 4 Black. Com. 272.

criminal. But since the passage of the Sts. 1858, ch. 138, § 1, and the Sts. 1877, ch. 211, § 1, justices of the peace have no power to try cases, civil or criminal, nor have they any power to receive complaints or to issue warrants except in certain cases.

§ 111. At the present time, in Massachusetts, the powers of justices of the peace are very limited, and are confined to certain ministerial acts, which are strictly defined by statutes.

APPOINTMENT.

§ 112. All justices of the peace shall be nominated and appointed by the governor, by and with the advice of the council ; and every such nomination shall be made by the governor, and made at least seven days prior to such appointment.[1]

§ 113. It is much easier to obtain the appointment of justice of the peace than that of notary public. Any man who is more than twenty-one years of age, of good character, a citizen of the United States and a resident of Massachusetts, may be appointed. But if the applicant is not a counsellor at law, it is better to allege good reasons for the appointment, on the application.

§ 114. Although women cannot be appointed justices of the peace, still women who are attorneys at law may be appointed special commis-

---

[1] Mass. Const., Part II. ch. ii. art. ix.

sioners, and shall have the same powers as justices of the peace for the following purposes: to administer all oaths which may be administered by a justice of the peace; to take depositions and affidavits; to take acknowledgments of deeds and other instruments; and to issue summonses for witnesses.[1]

§ 115. The applicant for the office must fill out a blank similar in form to the one below, and which may be procured at the office of the secretary of state. The application must be signed by two reputable citizens of the Commonwealth, and deposited in the executive office of the State House.

COMMONWEALTH OF MASSACHUSETTS.

To His Excellency the Governor:

hereby recommend , of [residence], [business address], for appointment to the office of justice of the peace for the Commonwealth of Massachusetts.

He is a citizen of the United States, a resident of Massachusetts, more than twenty-one years of age, and of high standing and character.

....

....

....189 .

---

[1] Sts. 1883, ch. 252; Sts. 1889, ch. 197.

§ 116. Every person appointed to the office of justice of the peace shall before the delivery of his commission pay to the secretary of the Commonwealth a fee of five dollars.[1]

§ 117. Every person appointed by the governor to the office of justice of the peace shall be notified by the secretary of the Commonwealth of his appointment, and if he does not, within three months from the date of such appointment, take and subscribe the oaths required to qualify him to execute the duties of the office to which he has been appointed, his appointment shall be null and void; and the secretary shall forthwith notify him thereof, and request him to return his commission to be cancelled, and shall also certify said facts to the governor.[2]

§ 118. The following oath shall be taken and subscribed by every person appointed to the office of justice of the peace, before he shall enter upon the duties of his office, to wit: —

I, A. B., do solemnly swear that I will bear true faith and allegiance to the Commonwealth of Massachusetts, and will support the Constitution thereof. So help me God.

Provided, that when any person shall be of the denomination called Quakers, and shall decline taking said oath, he shall make his affirmation in the foregoing form, omitting the word "swear,"

---

[1] Pub. Sts. ch. 21, § 6.   [2] Ibid., § 4.

and inserting instead thereof the word " affirm ; "
and omitting the words " So help me God," and
subjoining, instead thereof, the words, " This I do
under the pains and penalties of perjury."[1]

§ 119. Justices of the peace shall have jurisdiction and the right to act in all counties, except as
is stated in § 184, *post*, and hereafter all appoint-
ments of justices of the peace shall be made and
their commissions issued for the Commonwealth.[2]

§ 120. In order that the people may not suffer
from the long continuance in place of any justice
of the peace, who shall fail of discharging the
important duties of his office with ability or fidel-
ity, all commissions of justices of the peace shall
expire and become void, in the term of seven years
from their respective dates ; and upon the expiration of any commission, the same may, if necessary, be renewed, or another person appointed, as
shall most conduce to the well-being of the Commonwealth.[3]

§ 121. The secretary of the Commonwealth shall
send by mail to every person commissioned as a
justice of the peace, a notice of the time of the
expiration of his commission, not more than thirty,
nor less than fourteen days before such expiration.[4]

§ 122. A person who presumes to act as a justice of the peace after the expiration of his com-

---

[1] Mass. Const., Amend., Art. VI.   [2] Pub. Sts. ch. 155, § 5.
[3] Mass. Const., Part II. ch. iii. art. iii.
[4] Pub. Sts. ch. 15, § 14.

mission, and after receiving notice of such expiration sent as stated in the preceding section, shall
be punished by fine of not less than one hundred
nor more than five hundred dollars.[1]

MAY HOLD OTHER OFFICES.

§ 123. The office of justice of the peace is not
subject to the provisions regarding plurality of
office. So that a person may be a justice of the
peace, and at the same time hold any other office
which is within the gift of the governor of the
Commonwealth or that of the people.[2] A justice
of the peace may be a register in bankruptcy, or
may hold a judicial office under the laws of the
United States.[3] He shall be exempt from watch
and ward duties.[4]

§ 124. The governor with the advice and consent of the council shall from time to time designate and commission in the several counties a
suitable number of justices of the peace as trial
justices, and may at any time revoke such designation.[5]

FALSELY ASSUMING TO BE A JUSTICE.

§ 125. Whoever falsely assumes or pretends to
be a justice of the peace, and takes upon himself

[1] Pub. Sts. ch. 205, § 24.
[2] Mass. Const., Part II. ch. vi. art. ii. cl. 2; Amend., Art. VIII.
[3] Pub. Sts. ch. 160, §§ 14, 15.
[4] Ibid., ch. 34, § 6.   [5] Ibid., ch. 155, § 7.

to act as such, or to require any person to aid or assist him in a matter pertaining to the duty of such officer, shall be punished by imprisonment in the jail not exceeding one year, or by fine not exceeding four hundred dollars.[1]

[1] Pub. Stats. ch. 205, § 23.

CHAPTER II.

DEPOSITIONS.

METHOD OF TAKING.

§ 126. When a witness whose testimony is wanted in a civil cause or proceeding pending in this Commonwealth, lives more than thirty miles from the place of trial, or is about to go out of the Commonwealth and not to return in time for the trial, or is so sick, infirm or aged, as to make it probable that he will not be able to attend at the trial, his deposition may be taken as is hereinafter stated.[1]

§ 127. When a deposition is taken with a view to a future trial, it is always subject to contingencies. Therefore a deposition which is certified by the justice of the peace who took it that it was taken because the witness was about to go out of the Commonwealth, is admissible if the witness is out of the state at the time of the trial, although he testifies in the deposition that he has no present purpose of leaving the state.[2]

[1] Pub. Sts. ch. 169, § 24.
[2] Livesey v. Bennett, 14 Gray, 131.

§ 128. At any time after the cause is commenced by the service of process, or after it is submitted to arbitrators or referees, either party may apply to a justice of the peace, who shall issue a notice to the adverse party to appear before said justice or any other justice of the peace, at the time and place appointed for taking the deposition, and to put such interrogatories as he thinks fit.[1]

§ 129. The brother-in-law of one who as stake-holder is made a party to a suit in equity, is not disqualified to take a deposition in the case as a justice of the peace. The stakeholder has no interest in the suit, for he was merely a trustee for both parties, and his brother-in-law, the justice of the peace who took the deposition, cannot be said therefore to be related to any party in interest in the suit.[2]

§ 130. The notice may be served on the adverse party or his agent or attorney; and when there are several plaintiffs, defendants or parties, on either side, a notice served on either of them shall be sufficient.[3]

§ 131. Where an attorney puts his name on the record as attorney to one of the parties in an action, notice given to him of the taking of a deposition will be sufficient, the party whom he represents being estopped by the record to allege that he appeared without authority.[4]

---

[1] Pub. Sts. ch. 169, § 25. [2] Culver v. Benedict, 13 Gray, 7.
[3] Pub. Sts. ch. 169, § 26. [4] Smith v. Bowditch, 7 Pick. 137.

§ 132. The notice shall be served by delivering an attested copy thereof to the person to be notified, or by leaving such copy at his place of abode, not less than twenty-four hours before the time appointed for taking the deposition, and also allowing time for his travel to the place appointed, not less than at the rate of one day, Sundays excluded, for every twenty miles' travel.[1]

§ 133. The reading to the adverse party of a notice of the time and place appointed for the taking of a deposition, is not a legal service of such notice.[2]

§ 134. The object of the statute is very clear. The person notified shall have not less than twenty-four hours' notice before the time required for his attendance; and if he has to travel to the place of attendance, he shall have sufficient time for that purpose, not less than at the rate of one day for every twenty miles' travel. The time and distance are measured by hours, and therefore fractions of a day may be computed both as to notice and the time necessary to reach the place of appointment.[3]

§ 135. The general rule of law is, that every witness must give his evidence in person before the court and jury, so that they may be able to

---

[1] Pub. Sts. ch. 169, § 27.

[2] Young v. Capen, 7 Met. 287.

[3] Hubbard, J., in City Bank at Providence v. Fullerton, 11 Met. 78.

judge of his credibility by his appearance and manner of testifying. There are exceptions to this rule founded on considerations of convenience and necessity. But if a party desires to use the testimony of an absent witness, this can only be done by showing that the provisions of law regulating the mode of depositions have been complied with. If any essential requisite is omitted, the deposition, however full and accurate it may be in other respects, is not legal evidence. The intent of the statute was, in providing that the adverse party must have twenty-four hours' notice of the time for taking the deposition, that a party should not be suddenly called upon at the pleasure of his adversary to attend to the taking of material testimony, without having some time for preparation and to procure the attendance of counsel.[1]

Form of Notice to Adverse Party.

COMMONWEALTH OF MASSACHUSETTS.

S. } ss.

To A. B.,   of B., in the County of M., *Greeting.*

Whereas C. D., of W., in the County of M. has requested me to take the deposition of E. F. of R., in the County of E., to be used in an action of [tort or contract] pending between you and the said C. D. and the [house, office, or store] of G. H. in said R., and the

---

[1] Bigelow, C. J., in Hunt *c.* Lowell Gas Light Co., 1 Allen, 347.

day of   , in the year of our Lord one thousand
eight hundred and ninety-   , at   of the clock
in the   noon, are appointed the time and place for
the said deponent to testify what   he   know   relating
to said action.   You are hereby notified that you may
then and there be present, and put such interrogatories
as you may think fit.

Given under my hand and seal, at   , on the
        day of   , in the year of our Lord one
thousand eight hundred and ninety-   .

S. P.,
Justice of the Peace. } [SEAL.]

§ 136. Instead of the written notice before prescribed, the notice may be given verbally by the
justice taking the deposition, or it may be wholly
omitted if the adverse party or his attorney in
writing waives the right to it. But where the
adverse party does not appear to defend within
the time required by law, the justice may take the
deposition without giving any notice.[1]

§ 137. The deponent shall be sworn or affirmed
to testify the whole truth, and nothing but the
truth, relating to the cause for which the deposition is taken. He shall then be examined by the
justice, and the parties if they think fit, and his
testimony shall be taken in writing.[2]

---

[1] Pub. Sts. ch. 169, § 28 ; Sts. 1883, ch. 188, § 1.
[2] Pub. Sts. ch. 169, § 29.

§ 138. The party producing the deponent shall be allowed first to examine him, either upon verbal or written interrogatories, on all the points which he deems material; the adverse party may then examine him in like manner; after which either party may propose such further interrogatories as the case may require.[1]

§ 139. The deposition shall be written by the justice, or by the deponent, or by some disinterested person in the presence and under the direction of the justice, and it shall be carefully read to or by the deponent, and shall then be subscribed by him.[2]

§ 140. A deposition which is certified as made and subscribed by the deponent is sufficient, for the meaning seems to be that the deposition was written either by the deponent himself, or by the justice, or by some other person by the direction of the justice; and that it was read to or by the deponent. For if it were not so written and read, it would seem that the justice could not certify of his own knowledge that the deposition was made by the deponent.[3]

§ 141. Exhibits and documents annexed to a deposition are not required to be in the handwriting of the justice of the peace or of some person appointed by him. Thus it is no objection to a deposition that the bill of items of the plaintiff's

---

[1] Pub. Sts. ch. 169, § 30. [2] Ibid., § 31.
[3] Brown v. King, 5 Met. 183.

account annexed to the deposition, and sworn to by the deponent, is not in the handwriting of the justice of the peace who took the deposition, or of the deponent, or of some disinterested person.[1]

§ 142. The justice shall annex to the deposition a certificate of the time and manner of taking it, the person at whose request, the cause or suit for which it was taken, and the reason for taking it, and stating also whether the adverse party attended, and if not, stating the notice, if any, that was given to him.[2]

§ 143. The testimony of witnesses in the form of depositions cannot be received, unless there has been a full compliance with the actual and positive requirements of the law. Therefore if the certificate of the justice who took the deposition does not state that the deponent was sworn to tell the truth, the whole truth, and nothing but the truth, relating to the cause for which the deposition is taken, the law has not been complied with and the deposition will be of no effect.[3]

§ 144. It is the duty of a justice of the peace taking a deposition to state in his certificate " the reason for taking it; " but it is not necessary for the certificate to show in what manner or by what evidence the justice of the peace was satisfied of

---

[1] Marvin v. Raigan, 12 Cush. 132.

[2] Pub. Sts. ch. 169, § 32.

[3] Simpson v. Carleton, 1 Allen, 116; Hitchings v. Ellis, 1 Allen, 475; Bacon v. Rogers, 8 Allen, 146.

the existence of the cause for the taking. It is sufficient that he certifies to the fact upon his official responsibility.[1]

§ 145. If the certificate of a justice of the peace to a deposition shows that the deponent was sworn to testify in relation to an action pending between A. B. and C. D., it is sufficient, although it appears that another action with the same title is pending in the same court.[2]

§ 146. Where the deposition and the certificate are inclosed together, sealed up and directed to the clerk of the court by the justice of the peace, the certificate is annexed to the deposition within the meaning of the statute. If not the best, it is one method of annexation.[3]

Certificate of Justice to be annexed to Deposition.

COMMONWEALTH OF MASSACHUSETTS.

S. } ss.

This is to certify that E. F., the above-named deponent, appeared before me at   o'clock,   M., on the   day of   , A. D. 189 , at [state place], and gave the foregoing deposition, to be used in an action of [tort or contract] now pending between A. B., of B., in the county of M., and C. D., of W., in

---

[1] Littlehale *v.* Dix, 11 Cush. 365.
[2] Hale *v.* Silloway, 3 Allen, 358.
[3] Shaw *v.* McGregor, 105 Mass. 100.

the said county of M., before the   Court for the
county of   ; that prior to his examination the
said deponent was duly sworn by me to testify the
truth, the whole truth, and nothing but the truth, relating to the cause for which said deposition is taken ;
that both parties to the said action had an opportunity
to examine the said deponent as in the statute provided ;
that the said deposition was reduced to writing by me ;
that it was carefully read to the said deponent, and was
then subscribed by him ; that the said deposition was
taken at the request of the [plaintiff or defendant] in
said action, the said deponent being   , and that
the [plaintiff or defendant] in said action attended at
the taking of said deposition [if the adverse party did
not attend, state the notice, if any, that was given
him].

Dated at   this   day of   , A. D. 189 .

S. P.,
Justice of the Peace.

§ 147. The deposition shall be delivered by the
justice to the court, arbitrators, referees or other
persons before whom the cause is pending, or shall
be inclosed and sealed by him, and directed to
them, and shall remain sealed until opened by
them.[1]

§ 148. As the deposition with the annexed certificate is in the possession of the justice of the

---

[1] Pub. Sts. ch. 169, § 33.

peace until it is transmitted by him, he may correct any error or supply by additional statements any deficiency which he may discover in the caption. But after it has been delivered to the court or tribunal where it is to be used, the deposition is in their custody, and no alteration, change or amendment in the certificate of the justice of the peace accompanying it can be made without their order or permission.[1]

SUMMONING OF WITNESSES.

§ 149. A witness may be summoned and compelled to give his deposition at a place within twenty miles of his place of abode, in like manner and under the same penalties as he may be summoned and compelled to attend as a witness before a court.[2]

§ 150. A witness not having his place of abode in this Commonwealth, but being at the time herein, may be summoned and compelled to give his deposition at any place within ten miles of the place at which the summons is served upon him, in like manner and under the same penalties as he may be summoned and compelled to attend as a witness before a court.[3]

---

[1] Hitchings v. Ellis, 1 Allen, 476.
[2] Pub. Sts. ch. 169, § 38.   [3] Ibid., § 39.

Form of Deposition Summons.

COMMONWEALTH OF MASSACHUSETTS.

S. } ss.

To E. F. of R., in the county of E., *Greeting.*

Whereas C. D. of W. in the county of M., has requested me to take your deposition, to be used in an action now pending between him and A. B. of B., in the county of M.. and the [house, office, or store] of G. H. in said R., and the   day of   , in the year of our Lord one thousand eight hundred and at   of the clock in the   noon, are appointed the time and place for taking the same deposition.

You are hereby required, in the name of the Commonwealth of Massachusetts, then and there to appear, to testify what you know relating to the said action. Hereof fail not.

Given under my hand and seal, at   aforesaid, the   day of   , in the year of our Lord one thousand eight hundred and   .

S. T.,
Justice of the Peace. } [SEAL.]

§ 151. A witness may be summoned and compelled in like manner and under the same penalties as are prescribed in chapter 169 of the Public Statutes, to give his deposition in a cause pending in a court in any other state or government; which deposition may be taken before a justice of the peace in this

Commonwealth, or before commissioners appointed under the authority of the state or government in which the suit is pending ; and if the deposition is taken before such commissioners, the witness may be summoned and compelled to appear before them, by process from a justice of the peace in this Commonwealth.[1]

DEPOSITIONS TO PERPETUATE TESTIMONY.

§ 152. When a person is desirous to perpetuate the testimony of another person or of himself, he shall make a statement in writing setting forth briefly and substantially his title, claim or interest in or to the subject concerning which he desires to perpetuate the evidence, and the names of all other persons interested or supposed to be interested therein, and also the name of the witness proposed to be examined ; and shall deliver said statement to two justices of the peace, one of whom shall be either a judge or register of probate and insolvency, a clerk of the supreme judicial court, a master in chancery, or a counsellor at law, requesting them to take the deposition of said witness.[2]

§ 153. The justices shall thereupon cause notice to be given of the time and place appointed for taking the deposition to all persons mentioned in said statement as interested in the case. The notice shall be given in the manner prescribed in this

---

[1] Pub. Sts. ch. 169, § 44.　　　　[2] Ibid., § 45.

chapter respecting notice upon taking a deposition in this Commonwealth, to be used in a cause here pending; and when in the opinion of the justices no sufficient provision is made by law for giving notice to parties adversely interested, they shall cause such reasonable notice to be given as they deem proper.[1]

§ 154. If at the time and place appointed for taking the deposition the witness or a person interested appears and objects, the justices shall not proceed to take the same unless on hearing the parties it is made satisfactorily to appear that such testimony may be material to the petitioner, and is not sought for the purpose of discovery, or of using the same in a suit pending or thereafter to be brought against said witness, and that the petitioner is in danger of losing the same before it can be taken in any suit wherein his right, title, interest or claim can be tried. In all cases the petitioner, his agent or attorney shall, at the request of such witness or of a person interested in the deposition, be examined on oath in relation to the reasons for taking the same.[2]

§ 155. The deponent shall be sworn and examined, and his deposition shall be written, read and subscribed in the same manner as is prescribed respecting other depositions before mentioned; and the justices shall annex thereto a certificate under

---

[1] Pub. Sts. ch. 169, § 46.   [2] Ibid, § 47.

their hands of the time and manner of taking it, and that it was taken in perpetual remembrance of the thing; and they shall also insert in the certificate the names of the person at whose request it was taken, and of all persons who were notified to attend, and of all who did attend the taking thereof.[1]

Form of Certificate to be annexed to Deposition to Perpetuate Testimony.

COMMONWEALTH OF MASSACHUSETTS.

S. $\Big\}$ ss.

City [or town] of

This   day of   , in the year of our Lord eighteen hundred and ninety-   , personally appeared before us the subscribers, two justices of the peace for the said Commonwealth, the aforesaid deponent, and after being carefully examined and duly cautioned to testify the truth, the whole truth, and nothing but the truth, made oath [or affirmed] that the foregoing deposition by him subscribed is true. Taken at the request of   , to be preserved in perpetual remembrance of the thing. And we duly notified all persons living within twenty miles of this place of caption whom we knew to be interested in the property to which said deposition relates; and   attended [if any persons so notified did attend] [or, we not knowing any person

---

[1] Pub. Sts. ch. 169, § 48.

living within twenty miles of said place of caption, interested in the property whereunto the said deposition relates, did not notify any persons to attend].

S. T., { [judge or register of probate and insolvency, clerk of supreme court, master in chancery, or counsellor at law].

U. V.,
Justices of the Peace.

§ 156. The deposition with the certificate, and also the written statement of the party at whose request it was taken, shall within ninety days after the taking thereof be recorded in the registry of deeds in the county or district where the land lies, if the deposition relates to real estate, otherwise in the county or district where the parties or some of them reside.[1]

§ 157. A witness may be summoned and compelled to give his deposition in perpetual remembrance of the thing as before prescribed, in like manner and under the same penalties as are stated in this chapter respecting other depositions taken in this Commonwealth.[2]

DEPOSITIONS BY PARTIES.

§ 158. The testimony of parties may be taken or given by depositions, for the causes and in the man-

[1] Pub. Sts. ch. 169, § 49.   [2] Ibid., § 51.

ner provided for other witnesses, and the expenses of such depositions shall be taxed in the bill of costs as in the other cases.[1]

FEES.

§ 159. The fees of justices of the peace for taking a deposition shall be fifty cents; for writing the deposition and caption, at the rate of twelve cents a page of two hundred and twenty-four words; and for the notice to the adverse party, twenty cents; the justice shall certify on the deposition his own fees and those of the deponent, and where the attendance of two or more justices is required, each of them shall be entitled to the fees prescribed.[2]

[1] Pub. Sts. ch. 169, § 65.　　.　[2] Ibid., ch. 199, § 1.

CHAPTER III.[1]

CALLING OF MEETINGS.

CORPORATIONS.

§ 160. When by reason of the death, absence or other legal impediment of the officers of a corporation there is no person duly authorized to call or preside at a legal meeting, a justice of the peace may, on a written application of three or more of the members, issue a warrant to either of them, directing him to call a meeting by giving such notice as had been previously required by law; and the justice may in the same warrant direct such person to preside at the meeting until a clerk is duly chosen and qualified, if no officer is present legally authorized to preside.[2]

§ 161. The justice of the peace who issues a warrant on the application of three persons representing themselves as members of a corporation, does not pass upon the question whether such persons are legal members of such corporation, or whether

---

[1] Should the justice have occasion to issue warrants under §§ 160–172 and 174–176, he will find that the essential parts are stated with sufficient clearness in those sections.

[2] Pub. Sts. ch. 105, § 11.

such meeting is, when assembled, a legal one, and competent to act on the business for which it is assembled.[1]

§ 162. A justice of the peace upon the written request of a majority of the acting directors of a corporation may call a special meeting of the stockholders to confirm the legality of the organization of the corporation or of any of its proceedings, whether the corporation is formed under the general corporation law or under special statutes.[2]

AQUEDUCT CORPORATIONS.

§ 163. Persons who have associated by an agreement in writing to become proprietors of an aqueduct for the purpose of conveying fresh water into or within a city or town, or of funds for establishing such aqueduct, may apply in writing to a justice of the peace, stating the name and style of their association and the objects of their proposed meeting, and requesting him to call the same. The justice may thereupon issue his warrant stating the time, place and objects of the meeting, and directing some one of the persons applying to notify the same.[3]

FIRE DISTRICTS.

§ 164. If the selectmen, upon the application in writing of not less than seven freeholders, inhabi-

[1] Stevens v. Taft, 3 Gray, 489.   [2] Pub. Sts. ch. 106, §§ 79, 80.
[3] Ibid., ch. 110, § 1.

tants of a proposed fire district, requiring them to notify a meeting of the inhabitants of the district duly qualified to vote in town affairs, for the purpose of considering the expediency of organizing such district and establishing a fire department, shall refuse or neglect to notify such meeting, a justice of the peace may notify the same. The justice shall notify the meeting in the same manner that town meetings are notified.[1] (See § 173, *post.*)

GENERAL FIELDS.

§ 165. Upon the application of two or more proprietors of general fields to a justice of the peace, the latter shall issue his warrant to one of the applicants, directing him to call a meeting of the proprietors, and expressing in the warrant the time, place and purpose of the meeting.[2]

MEETING-HOUSE PROPRIETORS.

§ 166. A meeting of a corporation of proprietors of meeting-houses to alter, enlarge, repay, rebuild or remove the meeting-house, may be called by a warrant issued by a justice of the peace, on application in writing by any five of the members of the corporation, which warrant shall be directed to one of the applicants.[3]

---

[1] Pub. Sts. ch. 35, § 42. [2] Ibid., ch. 111, § 22.
[3] Ibid., ch. 38, § 32.

PRIVATE WAYS AND BRIDGE PROPRIETORS.

§ 167. A justice of the peace may issue his warrant for a meeting of proprietors of private ways and bridges, when four or more persons are the proprietors and rightful occupants of a private way or bridge, and three of them make application to such justice to call a proprietors' meeting. The warrant must set forth the time, place and purpose of the meeting, and shall be posted up in some public place of the town where the way or bridge is situated, seven days at least before the time appointed for the meeting.[1]

RELIGIOUS SOCIETIES.

§ 168. A justice of the peace may, upon the application of five or more of the qualified voters, call a meeting of a religious society, in the manner stated in the following section, if there are no assessors or committee, or if such officers unreasonably refuse to call a meeting.[2]

§ 169. Any justice of the peace may, upon application in writing by five or more of the qualified voters of a religious society, which is legally capable of becoming a corporation, and so desires, issue his warrant directed to some one of the applicants, stating the objects of the proposed meeting, and requiring him to warn the qualified voters of the society to meet at a time and place appointed in the warrant.

---

[1] Pub. Stats ch. 52, § 26.   [2] Ibid., ch. 38, § 11.

Upon due return of the warrant, the same or any other justice of the peace may preside at the meeting for the choice and qualification of a clerk.[1]

§ 170. Any ten or more persons, male or female, who desire to form a religious society, may make for that purpose an application in writing to a justice of the peace. Such justice may thereupon issue his warrant directed to one of the applicants, stating the objects of the proposed society, and requiring him to warn said persons to meet at a time and place appointed in the warrant.[2]

TRUSTEES OF METHODIST EPISCOPAL CHURCHES.

§ 171. The first meetings of the trustees of any society of the Methodist Episcopal Church or of the African Methodist Episcopal Church may be called by a justice of the peace upon the application of three or more of the trustees. The provisions stated in the three preceding sections and in Pub. Stats. ch. 38, in relation to the warning and organization of meetings of religious societies, shall, so far as the same are applicable, apply to meetings for the organization of such trustees.[3]

SOCIAL LIBRARY CORPORATIONS.

§ 172. Upon application of five or more proprietors of a social library corporation, a justice of the peace may issue his warrant to one of them,

---

[1] Pub. Sts. ch. 38, § 25.   [2] Ibid., ch. 38, § 26.   [3] Ibid., § 46.

directing him to call a meeting of the proprietors at the time and place and for the purpose expressed in the warrant.[1]

TOWN MEETINGS.

§ 173. If the selectmen of a town unreasonably refuse to call a town meeting, a justice of the peace, upon the application of ten or more legal voters of the town, may call such meeting by a warrant under his hand directed to the constables of the town, if there are any, or, if there is no constable, then to any of the persons applying therefor, directing them to summon the inhabitants qualified to vote in town affairs to assemble at the time and place and for the purposes expressed in the warrant.[2] During the election of a moderator at a town meeting, the justice of the peace calling such meeting, if the meeting is so called, and if neither the town clerk nor a selectman is present, shall preside. A justice of the peace, when so presiding, shall have the powers and perform the duties of a moderator.[3]

Application for a Town Meeting, when the Selectmen have declined to call one.

To S. T., Esq., a Justice of the Peace for the Commonwealth of Massachusetts:

The subscribers, residents in and legal voters of the town of M., in the county of P., show that application

---

[1] Pub. Sts. ch. 40, § 13.   [2] Sts. 1893, ch. 417, § 262.

[3] Ibid., § 263.

has been made to [here state the names of the select-
men], selectmen of said town, to call a meeting of the
inhabitants thereof, duly qualified to vote at town meetings [here state the purpose for which it was sought to
call the town meeting].

But said selectmen have unreasonably refused to call
a town meeting for those purposes. The said subscribers therefore request you to issue a warrant, as the law
in such cases directs, for calling a meeting of said
inhabitants for the purposes aforesaid.

Dated   , 189 .

(Signed) [by ten or more legal
voters of the town].

Warrant.

P.   } ss.

To W. H., one of the constables [or if there is no constable, then to one of the signers of the application]
of the town of M. in said county, *Greeting.*

Whereas A. B. and nine [or more] other residents in,
and legal voters of, the said town, have represented to
me the subscriber, a justice of the peace for the Commonwealth of Massachusetts, that application has been
made to [here state the names of the selectmen], selectmen of said town, to call a meeting of the inhabitants of
said town, qualified to vote in town meetings [here state
the purpose for which it was sought to call the town
meeting], but they have unreasonably refused to call a
meeting for those purposes, and have therefore made
application to me to call one for those purposes.

These are therefore, in the name of the Commouwealth of Massachusetts, to require you to notify the inhabitants of said town, qualified by law to vote in town affairs, to assemble at   , on   , the   day of   next, at   o'clock in the   noon, for the purposes above mentioned.

Given under my hand and seal this   day of   , in the year of our Lord eighteen hundred and ninety   .

S. T.,

Justice of the Peace.

WATCH DISTRICTS.

§ 174. A justice of the peace, in case of the refusal or neglect of the selectmen, may, upon the application in writing of not less than seven freeholders of a village which is competent to establish a watch district, the limits of which shall be defined in the application, requiring him to notify a meeting of the persons in such district qualified to vote in town affairs, for considering the expediency of establishing such watch district, forthwith give notice to such voters, in the manner in which notice of town meetings is given, to assemble at some suitable place within the district for said purpose, the substance of which shall be expressed in the notification.[1]

§ 175. When a village in which a watch district may be established belongs to two or more towns, the voters thereof may organize such district at a

---

[1] Pub. Sts. ch. 34, § 9.

meeting called and notified by a justice of the
peace, as is stated in the preceding section, to
whom application has been made by at least five
voters of each town who are inhabitants of such
district.[1]

PROPRIETORS OF WHARVES AND COMMON LANDS.

§ 176. Upon the application of five or more proprietors who hold in common lands, wharves or
other real estate, and who wish to form themselves
into a corporation, to a justice of the peace, such
justice shall issue his warrant to one of the
applicants directing him to call a meeting of all
the proprietors, and expressing in the warrant
the time, place, occasion and purpose of the
meeting.[2]

[1] Pub. Sts. ch. 34, § 10.   [2] Ibid., ch. 111, §§ 1, 2.

CHAPTER IV.

ACKNOWLEDGMENT OF DEEDS.

IN GENERAL.

§ 177. The acknowledgment of a deed shall be by the grantors or one of them, or by the attorney executing the deed, and, if made in this Commonwealth, shall be made before a justice of the peace or notary public: and the justice of the peace, before whom the acknowledgment is made, shall indorse a certificate of such acknowledgment upon the deed, or annex the same thereto.[1]

§ 178. Taking the voluntary acknowledgment of a deed under our statutes is a purely ministerial, and not a judicial act, nor in any way connected with a judicial proceeding. The general principles of law, the nature of the act and the language of the statute, all show that any justice of the peace may take an acknowledgment of a deed in any county within the state.[2]

§ 179. The only use of a certificate of a justice of the peace of the acknowledgment of a deed, is to

---

[1] Pub. Sts. ch. 120, § 6.
[2] Learned v. Riley, 14 Allen, 109.

entitle the deed to be recorded. The certificate is
not conclusive evidence that the grantor executed
the deed.[1]

Form of Acknowledgment of a Deed.

COMMONWEALTH OF MASSACHUSETTS.

S.　　　　} ss.　　　　　　　　189 .

Then personally appeared the above-named　　　　　,
and acknowledged the foregoing instrument to be
free act and deed, before me.

....

Justice of the Peace.

WHEN GRANTOR REFUSES TO ACKNOWLEDGE.

§ 180. If a grantor refuses to acknowledge his
deed, the grantee or any person claiming under
him may apply to a justice of the peace in the
county where the land lies or where the grantor or
a subscribing witness to the deed resides, and such
justice shall thereupon issue a summons to the
grantor to appear before him at a certain time and
place to hear the testimony of the subscribing witnesses ; which summons, with a copy of the deed
annexed, shall be served seven days at least before
the time therein assigned for proving the deed, and
at such hearing or any adjournment thereof the due

---

[1] O'Neil *r.* Webster, 150 Mass. 572.

execution of the deed may be proved by the testimony of one or more of the subscribing witnesses. The execution of a deed shall not be proved in the manner above stated, unless it has at least one subscribing witness.[1]

Application to a Justice of the Peace, when a Grantor or Lessor refuses to acknowledge a Deed, or a Lease for more then seven years.

COMMONWEALTH OF MASSACHUSETTS.

To S. T., Esq., a justice of the peace for the said Commonwealth.

Complains A. B. of   , that C. D. of   , on the   day of   , in the year of our Lord eighteen hundred and ninety   , signed and sealed a deed conveying to him [in fee simple, fee tail, for term of life, or lease for more than seven years, as the case may be]; [here the premises may be generally described], which deed the said C. D. has refused, and still continues to refuse, to acknowledge before a justice of the peace. He therefore requests you to issue a summons to the said C. D. to appear before you, to hear the testimony of the subscribing witnesses thereunto, and that such other proceedings may be had thereon as the law in such cases directs.

, 189 .

(Signed) A. B.

---

[1] Pub. Sts. ch. 120, §§ 9, 12.

Summons thereon.

COMMONWEALTH OF MASSACHUSETTS.

S. $\left.\right\}$ ss.

To C. D. of

Whereas A. B. of , has complained to me, a justice of the peace for the said Commonwealth, that on the day of , you signed and sealed a deed, conveying to him [in fee simple, fee tail, for term of life, or lease for more than seven years, as the case may be], [here describe the premises], a copy of which is hereto annexed. Which deed, he says, you have refused and still do refuse to acknowledge before a justice of the peace, and has therefore requested me to summon you to appear before me, to hear the testimony of the sub-scribing witnesses thereunto, and further to proceed thereon as the law in such cases directs.

I do therefore, in the name of the Commonwealth of Massachusetts, hereby notify and summon you to appear before me, on the day of , at o'clock in the noon, at in , in the said county of S., then and there to hear the testimony of the subscribing witnesses E. F. and G. H., that such proceedings may be had thereon as the law of the Commonwealth in such cases directs.

Given under my hand and seal this day of , in the year of our Lord 189 .

S. T.,
Justice of the Peace.

A certificate of the proof of the execution of a deed shall be indorsed upon the deed or annexed thereto by the justice of the peace before whom such proof is made, and the justice of the peace shall state in his certificate whether the grantor was present at the hearing.[1]

Certificate to be annexed.

COMMONWEALTH OF MASSACHUSETTS.

S.   } ss.

I hereby certify, that on this   day of   , in the year of our Lord eighteen hundred and ninety- . E. F. and G. H., [or E. F., one of] the witnesses whose names are subscribed to the [foregoing or within] deed [or lease for more than seven years, as the case may be], appeared before me the subscriber, a justice of the peace for the said Commonwealth, and made oath that they [or he, as the case may be] saw the above [or within] named C. D. sign and seal the above [or within] deed [or lease], and that they [or he, as the case may be] subscribed their names as witnesses thereunto at the same time, the said C. D. being present [or the said C. D., although duly summoned according to law, was not present, as the case may be] when they [or he] took the said oath.

S. T.,
Justice of the Peace.

---

[1] Pub. Sts. ch. 120, § 13.

ACKNOWLEDGMENT OF DEEDS CONVEYING PROPERTY OUTSIDE OF THE COMMONWEALTH.

§ 181. Justices of the peace in this Commonwealth may take acknowledgments of deeds conveying real estate situated outside of Massachusetts and in the following states and territories : California, Colorado (the certificate of the justice must be affixed, and also a certificate by the clerk of some court of record of the county, city, or district wherein the justice resides, under the seal of such court, that the justice certifying the acknowledgment is the officer he assumes to be, that he has authority by the laws of Massachusetts to take and certify such acknowledgment, and that his signature is genuine), Connecticut, District of Columbia (there must be a certificate of the register, clerk or other public officer having cognizance of the fact, under his official seal, that at the date of acknowledgment the justice was in fact a justice of the peace), Florida, Idaho, Illinois (the official character of the justice must be certified by the clerk of the county court), Indiana (the acknowledgment shall be certified by the clerk of the county court where the justice resides, and attested by the seal of the court), Iowa (a certificate of the official character of the justice and of the genuineness of his signature is required), Kansas (the acknowledgment must be accompanied by a certificate of the official character of the justice under the hand of the clerk of some court of record and seal of the court), Louisiana (the official character of the justice must be properly verified before a commissioner of the State), Maine, Michigan, Minnesota (the justice should state his official character in his certificate), Mississippi (the official character of the justice shall be certified under the seal of some court of record in his county), Montana (the official character of the justice must be certified under the seal of the court, tribunal or officer within and for the county in which the justice of the peace may be acting, which has cognizance of the official character of the justice), New Hampshire, North Dakota, Ohio, Rhode Island, South Dakota, Vermont. In Nebraska, Nevada, New York, North Carolina, Oregon, Pennsylvania, Washington, Wisconsin, and Wyoming, the acknowledgment must be accompanied by the certificate of the clerk of a court of record of the county having a seal, showing the official character and the genuineness of the signature of the justice.

OF SHARES OF STOCK.

§ 182. A justice of the peace shall receive acknowledgments of deeds of shares of stock which are sold by treasurers of corporations, because of the failure of the proprietors to pay the assessments due upon the shares.[1]

---

[1] Pub. Sts. ch. 106, § 45.

FEES.

§ 183. The fees of a justice of the peace for taking the acknowledgment of a deed by one or more grantors, if done at the same time, shall be twenty-five cents.[1]

[1] Pub. Sts. ch. 199, § 1.

CHAPTER V.

ISSUING OF WARRANTS.

IN CRIMINAL CASES.

(a) *Warrants.*[1]

§ 184. The governor, with the advice and consent of the council, may from time to time, upon the petition of the selectmen of a town included within the judicial district of a district or police court, and in which neither a justice nor the clerk of such court resides, designate and commission some justice of the peace residing in said town, who may issue warrants returnable to said court in criminal cases arising within such judicial district, and take bail therein.[2] The fee for issuing a warrant under this section shall be one dollar.[3]

§ 185. A justice of the peace who has been designated and commissioned, as is stated in the preceding section, with authority to issue warrants in criminal cases, may lawfully receive the complaints

---

[1] Forms for warrants of various kinds may be had at the clerk's office of the district or police court in the district of which the justice of the peace is commissioned to issue warrants and take bail.

[2] Sts. 1884, ch. 286.　　　　[3] Pub. Sts. ch. 199, § 1.

upon which such warrants are issued. Since the warrants cannot be issued without complaints, authority to receive complaints is implied from the authority to issue warrants.[1]

§ 186. A justice of the peace who has authority to issue warrants in criminal cases arising anywhere within a certain district, and whose residence falls within a new town formed by the incorporation of a part of an old town in the district, may continue to issue warrants in cases which arise within the new town, as well as elsewhere in the district.[2]

§ 187. A justice of the peace has no authority to direct his warrant to a private person, except where it is absolutely necessary, and where the necessity is expressed in the warrant; but he must direct to a sheriff, deputy-sheriff or a constable.[3]

§ 188. Upon complaint made to the justice of the peace that a criminal offence has been committed, he shall examine on oath the complainant and any witnesses produced by him; shall reduce the complaint to writing, and cause the same to be subscribed by the complainant, and if it appears that such offence has been committed, the justice of the peace shall issue a warrant reciting the substance of the accusation, and requiring the officer to whom it is directed forthwith to take the person

---

[1] Commonwealth *v.* Taber, 155 Mass. 5; Commonwealth *v.* O'Hanlon, ibid., 198.

[2] Commonwealth *v.* Brennan, 150 Mass. 63.

[3] Commonwealth *v.* Foster, 1 Mass. 493.

accused and bring him before the court which the justice of the peace has the power to issue warrants returnable to, to be dealt with according to law, and in the same warrant may require the officer to summon such witnesses as shall be therein named to appear and give evidence on the examination.[1]

§ 189. No justice of the peace not designated and commissioned as a trial justice shall have, or exercise power, authority or jurisdiction to try cases, civil or criminal, or receive complaints, or issue warrants, except as is stated in § 184, *ante*, and except that a justice of the peace, who is also a clerk or assistant clerk of a police, district or municipal court, may receive complaints and issue warrants, returnable before some trial justice, or police, district or municipal court, having jurisdiction of the examination of the person charged with the offence.[2]

(b) *Bail.*

§ 190. In cases where the offence charged in the warrant is not punishable by death or imprisonment in the state prison, the justice may admit the person arrested to bail by taking from him a recognizance with sufficient sureties for his appearance in the court within the judicial district of which the offence charged was committed.[3]

---

[1] Pub. Sts. ch. 212, § 15.   [2] Ibid., ch. 155, § 6.
[3] Ibid., ch. 212, § 21.

§ 191. The justice of the peace who so admits the person arrested to bail shall certify that fact upon the warrant, and shall deliver the same with the recognizance to the officer.[1]

IN OTHER CASES.

(a) *Entry by Board of Health.*

§ 192. When the board of health thinks it necessary for the preservation of the lives or health of the inhabitants to enter any land, building, premises or vessel within its town, for the purpose of examining into and destroying, removing or preventing a nuisance, source of filth or cause of sickness, and the board or any agent thereof sent for that purpose is refused such entry, any member of the board or such agent may make complaint under oath to two justices of the peace of the county, stating the facts of the case so far as he has knowledge thereof; and said justices may thereupon issue a warrant directed to the sheriff or any of his deputies, to such agent of the board, or to any constable of such town, commanding him to take sufficient aid, and at any reasonable time repair to the place where such nuisance, source of filth or cause of sickness complained of may be, and to destroy, remove or prevent the same, under the directions of the board.[2]

---

[1] Pub. Sts. ch. 212, § 22.
[2] Pub. Sts. ch. 80, § 27.

Form of the Warrant.

COMMONWEALTH OF MASSACHUSETTS.

S. $\Big\}$ ss.

To the Sheriff of our County of S., or any of his deputies, or any Constable of the city [or town] of B., or to T., agent of the Board of Health of the said city [or town] within our said county, *Greeting:*

Whereas complaint under oath is made to us, the subscribers, two of the justices of the peace for the said Commonwealth, by   , [a member or agent of, as the case may be], the board of health of the said city [or town] of B., that   of the said city [or town] of B. has caused to exist a [nuisance, cause of sickness, or source of filth, as the case may be], [here particularly describe the nuisance and state its locality], and the same nuisance does still keep up and continue. You are therefore, in behalf of said Commonwealth, commanded to take sufficient aid, and at any reasonable time to repair to said place where said [nuisance, source of filth or cause of sickness] exists, and to destroy, remove or prevent the same, under the directions of said board of health.

Given under our hands and seals, this   day of   , in the year of our Lord eighteen hundred and ninety   .

S. T., [SEAL.]
U. V., [SEAL.]
Justices of the Peace.

(b) *Entry of Premises of Gas Consumer.*

§ 193. If any officer or servant of a gas-light company, having been duly authorized in writing by an officer of the company, is prevented or hindered from entering premises lighted with gas supplied by such company, for the purpose of examining or removing the meters, pipes, fittings and works for supplying and regulating the supply of gas, and of ascertaining the quantity of gas consumed or supplied, such officer or servant may make complaint under oath to a justice of the peace, stating the facts so far as he has knowledge of them, and the said justice may thereupon issue a warrant directed to the sheriff or either of his deputies, or to a constable of the city or town where such company is located, commanding him to take sufficient aid, and to repair to said premises with such officer or servant.[1]

Form of the Warrant.

COMMONWEALTH OF MASSACHUSETTS.

S.   } ss.

To the Sheriff of the County of S., or any of his deputies, or any Constable of the city [or town] of B., within our said county,   *Greeting :*

Whereas complaint under oath is made to us, the subscribers, two of the justices of the peace for the said

---

[1] Pub. Sts. ch. 61, § 15.

Commonwealth, by T., an officer [or servant, as the case may be] of the C. Company, a corporation organized for the purpose of supplying gas to the inhabitants of the said city [or town] of B., said T. being duly authorized, in writing, by the [president, treasurer, agent or secretary] of the said company, that he has been prevented from entering the premises of D.. situated in said city [or town] of B. [here describe premises and state locality], for the purpose of [here state purpose for which entry to the premises was sought]. You are therefore, in behalf of the Commonwealth, commanded to take sufficient aid and to repair to said premises with said T., and cause him to enter for the purpose aforesaid.

Given under our hands and seals, this   day of   , in the year of our Lord eighteen hundred and ninety   .

S. T.,
U. V.,
Justices of the Peace.

(c) *Search for Liquor illegally kept.*

§ 194. If two persons of full age, and competent to testify, make complaint under oath or affirmation before a justice of the peace who is authorized to issue warrants in criminal cases, that they have reason to believe, and do believe, that any spirituous or intoxicating liquor, described in the complaint, is kept or deposited by a person named therein in a store, shop, warehouse, building, vehicle. steamboat. vessel or place, and is intended for

7

sale contrary to law, or has been brought into a
town or city in violation of the provisions of § 17
of chapter 100 of the Public Statutes, such justice
of the peace, upon its appearing that there is probable cause to believe said complaint to be true,
shall issue a warrant of search to any sheriff,
deputy-sheriff, city marshal, chief of police, deputy-
marshal, police officer or constable, commanding
him to search the premises in which it is alleged
such liquor is deposited, and to seize such liquor,
with the vessels in which it is contained, and all
implements of sale and furniture used, or kept and
provided to be used, in the illegal keeping or sale
of such liquor, and securely keep the same until
final action is had thereon, and return the warrant
with his doings thereon as soon as may be to the
court having jurisdiction in the place where such
liquor is alleged to be kept or deposited.[1]

*Form of Complaint to search for Intoxicating
Liquor.*

COMMONWEALTH OF MASSACHUSETTS.

M.   } ss.

To N. C., Esquire, a justice of the peace, authorized to
issue warrants in criminal cases in the town of B.
in the county of M.

J. S. and L. P., both of said B., and both being of
full age and competent to testify, in behalf of the Com-

[1] Pub. Sts. ch. 100, § 30; Sts. 1884, ch. 191; Sts. 1888, ch. 297, § 1.

monwealth of Massachusetts on oath complain that they
have reason to believe, and do believe, that intoxicating
liquors, to wit [here describe the liquors, as a certain
quantity of rum, being about, and not exceeding
gallons; a certain quantity of gin, etc., according to
the facts] on the   day of   , in the year
eighteen hundred and   , were and still are kept
and deposited by D. E., of said B., in a certain   ,
situate [here describe the building or other place, with
particulars of its location sufficient to identify it] in
said B., and occupied by said D. E., and which liquors
are intended by said D. E. for sale in this Commonwealth, said D. E. not being authorized to sell the
same in this Commonwealth or keep the same for sale,
for any purpose, by any legal authority whatever,
against the peace of the Commonwealth and the form
of the statute in such case made and provided; and
said complainants pray for a warrant to search said
          , described as aforesaid for liquors, and that
the same be declared to be forfeited, and that said D. E.
and all other persons claiming an interest in said liquors, may be summoned to appear before a court having
jurisdiction of the case, to show cause, if any they have,
why said liquors should not be declared forfeited. [If
the place intended to be searched is a dwelling-house,
and no tavern, store, grocery, eating-room or place of
common resort is kept therein, the complaint should
conclude as follows: —]

And I, J. S., one of the above complainants, on oath,
say that I have reason to believe, and do believe, that
intoxicating liquor, such as above mentioned, has been
sold in the house above mentioned [or has been taken

from the house above mentioned for the purpose of being sold] by the occupant of said house, contrary to law, within one month next before this day, and that said liquor above mentioned is now kept in said house for sale by D. E. contrary to law, and my belief aforesaid is founded on the following facts and circumstances [here let such facts and circumstances be stated].

J. S.
L. P.

Received and sworn to at said B., before me this day of   . in the year eighteen hundred and   ; and it appears to me that there is probable cause to believe the foregoing complaint to be true.

N. C., *Justice of the Peace.*

Form of Warrant to Search for and Seize Liquors unlawfully kept for Sale.

COMMONWEALTH OF MASSACHUSETTS.

M.   } ss.

To the Sheriff of our county of M., or either [L. S.]   of his deputies, or any Constable of the town of B., in said county,   *Greeting:*

Whereas J. S. and L. P., both of said B., and both of full age, and competent to testify, on the   day of   , in the year eighteen hundred and   , at said B., in behalf of the Commonwealth aforesaid, on oath complained to the undersigned. a justice of the peace authorized to issue warrants in criminal cases in said town of B., that they have reason to believe. and do believe, that on the   day of   , in the year eighteen hundred and   , at said B., intoxicating liquors, to wit: [here describe the liquors as in the complaint] are kept and deposited by D. E. of said B., in a certain   , situate [here describe the building or other place, as in the complaint] in said B., and occupied by said D. E. as a   , and that said liquors were. and are, intended for sale by the said D. E., in this Commonwealth, contrary to law, — he, said D. E., not being then and there authorized to sell or keep such liquors for sale in this Commonwealth for any purpose by any legal authority whatever : whereby said liquors have become forfeited.   [In case the place to be searched is a dwelling-house, and no tavern. store, grocery, eating-room or place of common resort is kept therein, the warrant should contain the following clause. But in a warrant for searching any other place besides a dwelling-house. the following clause should be omitted.]

(And J. S., one of the said complainants, has duly made oath that he has reason to believe, and doth believe, that intoxicating liquors, such as are mentioned in the complaint, have been illegally sold in said house. within one month last past, by the occupant thereof [or with the permission and consent of the occupant thereof, or have been taken from said house for the purpose of being sold] contrary to law, within one month last past. and that such liquors are kept and deposited in said house by said D. E., and intended for sale in this Commonwealth, contrary to law, and has, in his said oath. stated the following facts and circumstances on which his said belief was founded: [here let the facts and circumstances be repeated, as in the complaint.])

And said complainants have also prayed that due process may issue to search for said liquors, and that such further proceeding may be had in the premises as to law and justice in that behalf may appertain; and whereas it appears to me, the subscriber, on the complaint aforesaid, that probable cause has been shown for the issuing of a warrant of search thereupon : —

These, therefore, are to require you, in the name of the Commonwealth, taking with you proper assistants, forthwith to enter the   , herein above described, and make diligent and careful search for all the liquors herein above described, and if such liquors are found therein, to seize and convey the same, and the vessels which contain such liquors, and all implements of sale or furniture used, or kept and provided to be used, in the illegal keeping or sale of such liquors, to some place of safety, and safely keep the same, to await the final action and decision of the court upon said complaint.

Herein fail not, and make due return of this warrant, with your doings thereon.

Witness my hand and seal at said B., this day of   , in the year eighteen hundred and   .

N. C., *Justice of the Peace.*

(d) *Impounding Beasts.*

§ 195. When an owner or keeper of beasts is dissatisfied with the claim of the person impounding them, he may have the amount for which he is liable ascertained and determined by two dis-

interested and discreet persons, to be appointed
and sworn for that purpose by a justice of the
peace.[1]

FORMS.

*Warrant for ascertaining Damage done by Beasts taken
up and Impounded, to be issued at the request of
the Owners of such Beasts.*

To A. B. and C. D. of   , two disinterested and
   judicious persons,   *Greeting:*

You are hereby appointed and empowered faithfully
and impartially to estimate upon oath the damage done
to E. F. by [here describe the beasts], which for that
cause have been taken up by G. H. and impounded [here
state the pound and place where impounded].

Given under my hand this   day of   , in
the year of our Lord eighteen hundred and ninety

                          S. T.,
                   Justice of the Peace.

            Oath.

S.   } ss.

The above [or within] named A. B. and C. D. personally appeared and made oath that in estimating the
above [or within] mentioned damages, they would act
faithfully and impartially, according to their best skill
and judgment.

         Before me,   S. T.,
               Justice of the Peace.

---

[1] Pub. Sts. ch. 36, § 34.

Appraisers' Return.

B.   ,   189 .

Pursuant to the within warrant, we have considered the damage done by the beasts within mentioned, and do upon oath estimate the same at   .

A. B.
C. D.

§ 196. A justice of the peace on an application from the person who has impounded beasts, and who has not received the sum for which the beasts were impounded, within fourteen days after notice of the impounding had been given, shall issue a warrant to two disinterested and discreet persons to be appointed and sworn by such justice, to ascertain and determine the sum due from the owner or keeper of the beasts.[1]

FORMS.

Warrant for Estimating the Damages done by Beasts taken up and Impounded, to be issued on the application of the one who Impounded them.

To A. B. and C. D. of   , two disinterested and judicious persons,   *Greeting:*

You are hereby appointed and empowered faithfully and impartially to estimate upon oath the damage done to E. F. by [here describe the beasts], which for that cause have been taken up and impounded by G. H. [in

---

[1] Pub. Sts. ch. 36, § 35.

such pound or in such place], and also in like manner
to appraise so many of the said beasts as shall be sufficient to answer the said damages and all charges.

Given under my hand this   day of   , in
the year of our Lord eighteen hundred and ninety   .

S. T.,
Justice of the Peace.

Oath.

S.   } ss.

The above [or within] named A. B. and C. D. personally appeared and made oath, that in estimating the
within [or above] mentioned damages and appraising
any of the within mentioned beasts, they would act
faithfully and impartially, according to their best skill
and judgment.

Before me,   S. T.,
Justice of the Peace.

Appraisers' Return.

Pursuant to the within warrant, we have considered
the damage done by the beasts within mentioned, and
do upon oath estimate the same at   .

We have also appraised the following beasts [or the
said beasts] to answer said damages [here insert the
kind and price].

A. B.
C. D.

(e) *Infected Articles.*

§ 197. When upon application of the board of health, it appears to a justice of the peace that there is just cause to suspect that baggage, clothing or goods, found within the town, are infected with the plague or other disease dangerous to the public health, he shall, by warrant directed to the sheriff or his deputy, or to any constable, require him to impress so many men as said justice may judge necessary to secure such baggage, clothing or goods, and to post said men as a guard over the house or place where such articles are lodged.[1]

§ 198. The justice may by the same warrant, if it appears to him necessary, require the officers, under the direction of the board of health, to impress and take up convenient houses or stores for the safe keeping of such articles.[2]

FORM

of the Warrant.

S.   } ss.

To the Sheriff of our County of S., or any of his deputies. or any Constable of the city [or town] of B., within our said county,   *Greeting :*

It appearing to me the subscriber, a Justice of the Peace for the Commonwealth of Massachusetts, upon

---

[1] Pub. Sts. ch. 80. § 44.   [2] Ibid., § 45.

application of the board of health of said town, that there is just cause to suspect that [baggage, clothing or goods] at   , within said town, are infected with [here state the disease] dangerous to the public health. You are hereby directed, in the name of the said Commonwealth, to impress [here state the number] men and secure said [baggage, clothing, or goods], and to post said men as a guard over [here state the place where the articles are], and to take up, under the direction of said board of health, such houses or stores as may be convenient for the keeping of said articles.

Given under my hand and seal, this   day of   , in the year of our Lord eighteen hundred and ninety   .

S. T.,
Justice of the Peace.

(f) *Lost Goods, Appraisals.*

§ 199. A justice of the peace, upon application of a finder of lost goods or stray beasts of the value of ten dollars or more, shall issue a warrant directed to two disinterested persons, to be appointed by such justice, and returnable into the office of the clerk of the city or town within seven days from date, requiring them to appraise the lost goods or stray beasts at their true value. Such persons shall be sworn by the justice.[1]

---

[1] Pub. Sts. ch. 95, § 4.

FORM.

Warrant to appraise Lost Goods or Stray Beasts.

S.   } ss.

To E. B. of   , and C. D. of   , two disinterested and judicious persons,   *Greeting:*

By virtue of the power and authority to me given, in
and by section four of chapter ninety-five of the Public
Statutes, I do hereby appoint you to appraise upon oath,
at the true value thereof in money, according to your
best skill and judgment, [here mention the goods or
beasts found] found by E. F. at   , and of the
value of ten dollars or more. Having performed this
service, you are to make return of this warrant into
the clerk's office of said G. within seven days from the
date hereof.

Given under my hand and seal, this   day of
   , in the year of our Lord eighteen hundred and
ninety

                           S. T.,
                     Justice of the Peace.

Oath.

S.   } ss.   189 .

The above named E. B. and C. D. personally appeared
and made oath, that they would faithfully and impartially perform the service to which they are appointed
by the above warrant.

         Before me,   S. T.,
                     Justice of the Peace.

§ 200. A justice of the peace, in case of disagreement between the owner and the finder of lost goods, as to what are the proper charges for the former to pay to the latter, shall determine the amount of the charges.[1]

(g) Removal of Sick Persons.

§ 201. Two justices of the peace may, if need be, make out a warrant directed to the sheriff of the county or his deputy, or to any constable, requiring them under the direction of the board of health to remove any person infected with contagious sickness, or to impress and take up convenient houses, lodging, nurses, attendants and other necessaries for the accommodation, safety and relief of the sick.[2]

FORM

of the Warrant.

S. } ss.

To the Sheriff of our County of S., or any of his deputies, or any Constable of the city [or town] of B., within our said county, *Greeting:*

Whereas complaint is made to us the subscribers, two of the justices of the peace for the Commonwealth of Massachusetts, by the board of health of said city [or town] of B., that   are [or is] sick with   , at the house of   in said town, and ought to be

---

[1] Pub. Sts. ch. 95, § 5.   [2] Ibid., ch. 80, § 43.

removed therefrom for the safety of the public health.
You are hereby required, in the name of the Commonwealth of Massachusetts, with the advice and under the
direction of the board of health of the said city [or
town] of B., [to remove   from the house of   ,
in said town, to   ], or [to impress] [here state
the articles which are judged necessary for the accommodation, or safety and relief, of the said   ,
as the case may be].

Given under our hands and seals, this   day of
          , in the year of our Lord eighteen hundred and
ninety   .

S. T.,
U. V.,
Justices of the Peace.

(h) *Fees.*

§ 202. The fees of justices of the peace for
granting a warrant of appraisement of lost goods
or stray beasts, and in all other cases, shall be
twenty cents, and where two or more justices are
required to act, each is entitled to the prescribed
fees.[1]

[1] Pub. Sts. ch. 199, § 1.

CHAPTER VI.

OATHS AND AFFIDAVITS.

IN GENERAL.

§ 203. Justices of the peace may administer oaths or affirmations in all cases in which an oath is required, unless a different provision is expressly made by law.[1]

§ 204. The usual mode of administering oaths now practised in this Commonwealth, with the ceremony of holding up the hand, shall be observed in all cases in which an oath may be administered by law.[2]

AGE AND SCHOOLING CERTIFICATES.

§ 205. A justice of the peace may administer the oath provided for in the Age and Schooling certificate of 1888, as follows : —

Age and Schooling Certificate. Law of 1888.

This certifies that I am the [father, mother, or guardian] of [name of child], and that [he or she] was born at [name of town or city], in the county of [name

---

[1] Pub. Sts. ch. 155, § 2.   [2] Ibid., ch. 169, § 13.

of county, if known], and state [or country] of [name], on the [day and year of birth], and is now [number of years and months] old.

  [Signature of father, mother, or guardian.]

[Town or city and date.]

  Then personally appeared before me the above named [name of person signing], and made oath that the foregoing certificate by [him or her] signed is true to the best of [his or her] knowledge and belief.

       Justice of the Peace.[1]

COLLECTORS OF TAXES.

 § 206. Justices of the peace shall receive the affidavits of collectors of taxes of the service of notice on the purchaser of real estate at a sale for non-payment of taxes, that the tax title is invalid, and also affidavits of the publication of such notice; affidavits of collectors of taxes of the posting and publishing notices of intention to take real estate for taxes; and affidavits of collectors of taxes, of no bid, and of the non-payment of bidders at sales of real estate for the non-payment of taxes.[2]

NOTARIES PUBLIC AND BANK OFFICERS.

 § 207. Justices of the peace shall receive the oaths of notaries' public and bank officers that

[1] Sts. 1888, ch. 348, §§ 4, 5.
[2] Sts. 1888, ch. 390, §§ 67, 70; Sts. 1892, ch. 109, § 1.

the statements which they have made concerning the contents of safety deposit vaults which have been opened for non-payment of rent, are true.[1]

NOTICES OF SALES OF PEWS.

§ 208. An affidavit of a notice of sales of pews in a church for the non-payment of assessments, in order to be allowed as a mode of proof of the posting up of the notification, must be made before a justice of the peace.[2]

OFFICERS OF RELIGIOUS SOCIETIES.

§ 209. A justice of the peace may administer the oaths of office to the clerks, assessors, treasurers and collectors of religious societies. Such oaths shall be substantially the same as are required to be taken by the clerk, assessors and collectors of towns.[3]

PEDLERS.

§ 210. Justices of the peace shall certify the oaths of pedlers that they are the persons named in their certificates, and that they are, or have declared their intention to become, citizens of the United States.[4]

---

[1] Sts. 1887, ch. 89.   [2] Pub. Sts. ch. 38, § 35.
[3] Ibid., ch. 38, § 14.   [4] Ibid., ch. 68, § 4.

RAILROAD POLICE.

§ 211. Railroad police officers shall be sworn before any justice of the peace.[1]

INSPECTION OF PEDLERS' LICENSES.

§ 212. Justices of the peace may command pedlers to exhibit to them their licenses. The licenses are granted for the term of one year by the secretary of the Commonwealth; they must contain the names of the cities and towns which the pedler selects, with the sums to be paid to the respective treasurers; they may be granted for the sale of any goods, wares or merchandise, except jewelry, wines, spirituous liquors, playing cards, indigo and feathers.[2]

FEES.

§ 213. The fee of a justice of the peace for administering an oath required by law, except on a trial or examination before himself, whether to one or more persons at the same time, shall be twenty-five cents.[3]

---

[1] Sts. 1883, ch. 65.   [2] Pub. Sts. ch. 68, §§ 13, 3–5.
[3] Ibid., ch. 199, § 1.

CHAPTER VII.

GENERAL POWERS AND DUTIES.

APPOINTMENT OF APPRAISERS.

§ 214. A disinterested justice of the peace may appoint appraisers of any part of the estate of a deceased person, which may be in the county in which such justice resides. The appraisers shall be three in number, and shall be sworn to the faithful discharge of their duties. The justice of the peace who has appointed the appraisers, shall issue an order to them, in substance as follows: —

} ss.

To   , of   in said county. You are hereby appointed to appraise on oath the estate and effects of   , late of   , deceased, which may be in said county. When you have performed that service, you will deliver this order and your doings in pursuance thereof to   , executor [or administrator, as the case may be] of said deceased, that he may return the same to the probate court for the county of   .

Given under my hand this   day of   , in the year   .

Justice of the Peace.[1]

[1] Pub. Sts. ch. 132, §§ 6, 7.

§ 215. The fee of a justice of the peace for granting a warrant of appraisement of the estate of a deceased person, shall be twenty cents.[1]

ARBITRATION.

§ 216. All controversies which might be the subject of a personal action at law or of a suit in equity may be submitted to the decision of one or more arbitrators in the following manner : —

The parties to all controversies which might be the subject of a personal action at law or of a suit in equity, and who wish to settle such controversies by submitting them to the decision of one or more arbitrators, shall appear in person, or by their lawful agents or attorneys, before a justice of the peace, and shall there sign and acknowledge an agreement in substance as follows : —

Know all men that   , of   , and   , of   , hereby agree to submit the demand, a statement whereof is hereto annexed [and all other demands between them, as the case may be], to the determination of   and   , the award of whom, or of the greater part of whom, being made and reported within one year from this day to the superior court for the county of   , the judgment thereon shall be final ; and if either of the parties neglects to appear before the arbitrators, after due notice given him of the

---

[1] Pub. Sts. ch. 199, § 1.

time and place appointed for hearing the parties, the arbitrators may proceed in his absence.

Dated this   day of   , in the year   .

....

The justice, who may be one of the arbitrators, shall subjoin to the agreement his certificate, in substance as follows : —

}ss.

Then the above named   and   personally appeared [or the above named   personally, and said   by   , his attorney, appeared, as the case may be], and acknowledged the above instrument by them signed to be their free act. Before me,

Justice of the Peace.[1]

§ 217. Reasonable compensation to arbitrators appointed under the provisions stated in the preceding section, upon whose award judgment is entered, shall be awarded by the supreme court.[2] The fees of a justice of the peace in a reference to arbitration, for the agreement of submission and acknowledgment, shall be forty cents.[3]

§ 218. A submission to arbitration to which a partnership is one party, must show who are

[1] Pub. Sts. ch. 188, §§ 1, 2.
[2] Sts. 1886, ch. 51, § 1 ; Sts. 1887, ch. 289, § 1.
[3] Pub. Sts. ch. 188, § 13.

members of the firm,[1] and when a submission to arbitration entered into before a justice of the peace, is signed by several partners on the one part, it must be acknowledged by all of the partners who signed it.[2]

ARREST ON MESNE PROCESS.

§ 219. A justice of the peace, except in the county of Suffolk, may receive the affidavit of a plaintiff who is seeking to arrest a person on mesne process in an action of contract. The plaintiff must make affidavit and prove to the satisfaction of the justice of the peace, the following statements : —

First, That he has good cause of action, and reasonable expectation of recovering a sum amounting to twenty dollars, exclusive of all costs which have accrued in any former action ;

Second, That he believes and has reason to believe that the defendant has property, not exempt from being taken on execution, which he does not intend to apply to the payment of the plaintiff's claim ; and,

Third, that he believes and has reason to believe that the defendant intends to leave the state, so that execution, if obtained, cannot be served upon him ;

Or (instead of the second and third) that the defendant is an attorney at law, that the debt

---

[1] Wesson v. Newton, 10 Cush. 114.
[2] Abbott v. Dexter, 6 Cush. 108 ; Horton v. Wilde, 8 Gray, 425.

sought to be recovered is for money collected by the defendant for the plaintiff, and that the defendant unreasonably neglects to pay the same to the plaintiff.

The justice of the peace must certify that he is satisfied that the allegations in the affidavit are true.[1]

§ 220. A justice of the peace, except in the county of Suffolk, may receive the affidavit of a plaintiff who is seeking to arrest a person in an action of tort, that he believes that he has a good cause of action against the defendant, that he has reasonable expectation of recovering a sum equal, at least, to one-third the damages claimed in the writ, and that he believes and has reason to believe that the defendant intends to leave the state, so that if execution be obtained it cannot be served upon him.

These allegations in the affidavit must be proved to the satisfaction of the justice of the peace, and he must certify that he is satisfied that they are true.[2]

§ 221. The fees of the justice of the peace for hearing an application for a certificate to arrest on mesne process in actions of tort or of contract, shall be one dollar.[3]

POWERS AS CONSERVATORS OF THE PEACE.

§ 222. Justices of the peace may. as conservators of the peace, upon view of an affray, riot, assault

---

[1] Pub. Sts. ch. 162, § 1.   [2] Ibid., § 2.   [3] Ibid., § 68.

or battery within their respective counties, without
a warrant in writing, command the assistance of
every sheriff, deputy-sheriff and constable, and of
all other persons present, for suppressing the same,
and for arresting all who are concerned therein,
as provided in chapters two hundred and eleven
and two hundred and twelve of the Public Statutes.
Persons so arrested shall be brought before some
police, district or municipal court, or trial justice
for examination.[1]

§ 223. If a prisoner, lawfully arrested without
a warrant by order of a justice of the peace, for
an assault committed in his presence, as is stated
in the preceding section, escapes, the justice of the
peace may order a constable to pursue and retake
the offender without a warrant. The justice of
the peace has the same authority to command assistance in pursuing and retaking an offender
whom he has caused to be arrested for an offence
committed in his presence and who has escaped,
that he has to command assistance in making the
original arrest.[2]

§ 224. Powers of determination and action of a
quasi judicial character are given to justices of the
peace by the statute stated in § 222 *ante*, which
from their nature must be exercised finally and
conclusively, without a hearing or even notice to
the parties who may be affected.[3]

[1] Pub. Sts. ch. 155, § 1.   [2] Com. *v.* McGahey, 11 Gray, 194.
[3] Salem *v.* Eastern Railroad Co., 98 Mass. 444.

§ 225. Whoever, being required by a justice of the peace, upon view of a breach of the peace or any other offence proper for his cognizance, to apprehend the offender, refuses or neglects to obey such justice, shall be punished in the manner provided in Pub. Sts. ch. 205, § 21, for refusing assistance to a sheriff; and no person to whom such justice is known or declares himself to be a justice of the peace, shall plead any excuse on pretence of ignorance of his office.[1]

§ 226. If persons to the number of twelve or more, being armed with clubs or other dangerous weapons, or if persons to the number of thirty or more, whether armed or not, are unlawfully, riotously or tumultuously assembled in a city or town, it shall be the duty of every justice of the peace living in any such city or town, to go among the persons so assembled, or as near to them as may be with safety, and in the name of the Commonwealth to command all the persons so assembled immediately and peaceably to disperse; and if such persons do not thereupon immediately and peaceably disperse, it shall be the duty of each of said magistrates and officers to command the assistance of all persons there present in seizing, arresting and securing such persons in custody, so that they may be proceeded with for their offence according to law.[2]

---

[1] Pub. Sts. ch. 205, § 22.
[2] Ibid., ch. 206. § 1.

§ 227. If a justice of the peace having notice of any such riotous or tumultuous and unlawful assembly in the city or town in which he lives, neglects or refuses immediately to proceed to the place of such assembly or as near thereto as he can with safety, or omits or neglects to exercise the authority with which he is invested by Pub. Sts. ch. 206, for suppressing such assembly, and for arresting and securing the offenders, he shall be punished by fine not exceeding three hundred dollars.[1]

§ 228. If any persons who are so riotously or unlawfully assembled, and who have been commanded to disperse, as before provided, refuse or neglect to disperse without unnecessary delay, any two justices of the peace may require the aid of a sufficient number of persons, in arms or otherwise, as may be necessary, and shall proceed, in such manner as in their judgment is expedient, forthwith to disperse and suppress such assembly, and seize and secure the persons composing the same, so that they may be proceeded with according to law.[2]

§ 229. If by reason of the efforts made by any two justices of the peace or by their direction to disperse such assembly, or to seize and secure the persons composing the same, who have refused to disperse, though the number remaining may be less than twelve, any such person or any other person then present is killed or wounded, the jus-

---

[1] Pub. Sts. ch. 206, § 3.   [2] Ibid., § 4.

tices of the peace, and all persons acting by their order or under their directions, shall be held guiltless, and fully justified in law; and if any of said justices of the peace, or any person acting under or by their direction, is killed or wounded, all persons so assembled, and all other persons who, when commanded or required, refused to aid and assist said justices of the peace, shall be held answerable therefor.[1]

NOT TO BUY CERTAIN DEMANDS FOR COLLECTION.

§ 230. Justices of the peace shall not directly or indirectly buy or be interested in buying, or directly or indirectly lend or advance, or agree to lend or advance any money or other goods, or give or promise any valuable consideration whatever to any person, as an inducement to place or in consideration of having placed in the hands of any person any bond, note, book-debt or right of action for collection, with intent to make themselves any gain from the fees arising from such collection by a suit at law; and a justice of the peace who commits any of the above described offences, shall for each offence forfeit not less than twenty nor more than five hundred dollars.[2]

COMPLAINTS UNDER DOG LAWS.

§ 231. A justice of the peace shall take the oath of a person that he has been assaulted by a dog, or

---

[1] Pub. Sts. ch. 206, § 6.   [2] Ibid., ch. 160, §§ 6, 7.

thát he has found a dog strolling out of the enclosure or immediate care of its owner or keeper, and that he suspects the dog to be dangerous or mischievous, if given within forty-eight hours after such assault or finding, and the justice shall also give to such person a certificate of such oath signed by him.[1]

Complaint of one who has been Assaulted by a Mischievous Dog.

To S. T., Esq., a Justice of the Peace for the Commonwealth of Massachusetts.

Complains upon oath E. B. of   , that within forty-eight hours last past he has been suddenly assaulted, while he was quietly and peaceably walking [or riding] from   to   , in the county of S., by a dog belonging to [or in the keeping of] C. D. of   ; the same dog then and there being out of the enclosure [or immediate care] of the said C. D., and that he really suspects that the said dog is dangerous and mischievous.

B.   , 189 .

(Signed)   E. B.

S.   } ss.   , 189 .

The above named E. B. personally appeared and made oath to the truth of the above complaint by him signed.

Before me,   S. T.,
Justice of the Peace.

---

[1] Pub. Sts. ch. 102, § 95.

Complaint respecting a Dog found out of the Enclosure of its Owner.

To S. T., Esq., a Justice of the Peace for the Commonwealth of Massachusetts.

Complains upon oath E. B. of   , that within forty-eight hours last past he found a dog, which he really suspects to be dangerous and mischievous, strolling out of the enclosure of   , the owner [or out of the immediate care of   , the keeper] of said dog, at   in

B.   , 189 .

(Signed)   E. B.

S.   } ss.   , 189 .

The above named E. B. personally appeared and made oath to the truth of the above complaint by him signed.

Before me,   S. T.,
          Justice of the Peace.

Certificate to be given to one who has been Assaulted by a Mischievous Dog.

S.   } ss.   , 189 .

I hereby certify, that on this   day of   . in the year of our Lord eighteen hundred and ninety   , personally came before me the subscriber, a Justice of the Peace for the Commonwealth of Massachusetts, E. B. of   , in said county, and made oath, that within forty-eight hours last past he has been suddenly assaulted, while he he was quietly and peaceably walking [or riding] from   to   , at   , in said county, by a dog belonging to [or in the keeping of] C. D. of   ; the same dog being then and there out of the enclosure [or immediate care] of the said C. D., and that he really suspects that the said dog is dangerous and mischievous.

It is therefore the duty of the said C. D., agreeably to a law of the Commonwealth in such cases made and provided, forthwith to kill or confine the said dog.

S. T.,
Justice of the Peace.

Certificate respecting a Dog found out of the Enclosure of its Owner.

S.   } ss.   , 189 .

I hereby certify, that on this   day of   , in the year of our Lord eighteen hundred and ninety   , personally came before me the subscriber, a Justice of the Peace for the Commonwealth of Massachusetts, E. B. of   , in said county, and made oath. that within forty-eight hours last past he found a dog which he really suspects to be dangerous and mischievous, strolling out of the enclosure of   , the owner [or out of the immediate care of   , the keeper] of said dog, at   , in   .

It is therefore the duty of the said C. D., agreeably to a law of the Commonwealth in such cases made and provided, forthwith to kill or confine the said dog.

S. T.,
Justice of the Peace.

DETERMINATION OF AMOUNT DUE FOR EQUITY OF REDEMPTION.

§ 232. When lands or rights are taken and set off or sold on execution, the debtor may in all cases cause the amount due for redemption to be ascertained at his own expense by three justices of the peace in the manner following : One of the justices shall be chosen by the debtor, one by the creditor, and the third by the two first chosen ; or if the creditor neglects to choose one, the justice chosen by the debtor shall appoint the other two. After a hearing and examination of the case before the three justices, they or any two of them shall make and sign a certificate of the sum which they adjudge to be due for the redemption of the premises, which certificate shall be final and conclusive between the parties. The debtor may then make a tender of the sum so adjudged to be due, which shall be valid and effectual, notwithstanding he has made a previous tender of a different sum.[1]

FORECLOSURES OF MORTGAGES.

§ 233. A certificate of two competent witnesses to prove an entry without a judgment for breach of a condition of a mortgage, shall be made and sworn to before a justice of the peace.[2]

---

[1] Pub. Sts. ch. 172, § 33.　　　　[2] Ibid., ch. 181, § 2.

§ 234. A certificate of the entry of a mortgagee, for the purpose of foreclosure, sworn to before himself as a justice of the peace, is invalid. It is as contrary to elementary principles of justice to allow a justice of the peace to administer the requisite oath to such a certificate of his own entry under a mortgage to himself, as to permit him to take in his official capacity a deposition in a suit to which he is a party, or an acknowledgment of a deed to himself, or a recognizance for a debt due to him personally.[1]

HABEAS CORPUS.

§ 235. Every person imprisoned or restrained of his liberty, except in the cases mentioned in the following section, may as of right and of course prosecute a writ of *habeas corpus*, according to the provisions of chapter 185 of the Public Statutes, to obtain relief from such imprisonment or restraint, if it proves to be unlawful.[2]

§ 236. The following persons shall not be entitled as of right, to demand and prosecute said writ : —

First, Persons committed for treason or felony, or on suspicion thereof, or as accessories before the fact to a felony, when the cause is plainly and specially expressed in the warrant of commitment.

---

[1] Judd *v.* Tryon, 131 Mass. 345.
[2] Pub. Sts. ch. 185, § 1.

Second, Persons convicted or in execution upon legal process, civil or criminal.

Third, Persons committed on mesne process in a civil action on which they were liable to be arrested and imprisoned, unless when excessive and unreasonable bail is required.[1] The writ of *habeas corpus* may be granted in poor debtor proceedings.[2]

§ 237. The writ may be issued by a justice of the peace if there is no judge of the supreme judicial court, of the superior court, or of a probate police, district or municipal court who is known to said justice of the peace to be within five miles of the place where the party is imprisoned or restrained; and the writ may be issued by said justice of the peace, without regard to the county in which is the place of imprisonment.[3]

§ 238. When a writ of *habeas corpus* is issued by a justice of the peace, it should appear on the face of the writ, or else on the face of the petition when it is annexed to the writ, that the case exists in which authority is given to a justice of the peace to issue the writ. That is, it should appear that no judge of the supreme or superior courts, or of a probate, police, district or municipal court is known to the justice of the peace to be within five miles of the place where the party is imprisoned or restrained.[4]

§ 239. Application for the writ shall be made to the justice of the peace authorized to issue the

---

[1] Pub. Sts. ch. 185, § 2.   [2] Sts. 1888, ch. 419, § 12.
[3] Pub. Sts. ch. 185, § 3.   [4] Com. v. Moore, 19 Pick. 339.

same by complaint in writing, signed by the party for whose relief it is intended, or by some person in his behalf, and setting forth —

First, The persons by whom, and the place where the party is imprisoned or restrained, naming the prisoner and the person detaining him if their names are known, and describing them if their names are not known.

Second, The cause or pretence of such imprisonment or restraint, according to the knowledge and belief of the person applying.

Third, if the imprisonment or restraint is by virtue of a warrant or other process, a copy of such warrant or process shall be annexed, unless it is made to appear that such copy has been demanded and refused, or that by some sufficient reason a demand therefor could not be made. The facts set forth in the complaint shall be verified by the oath of the person making the application or of some other credible witness.[1]

§ 240. The justice of the peace to whom the complaint is made shall without delay award and issue a writ of *habeas corpus*, substantially in the form heretofore established and used in this Commonwealth, and returnable forthwith at such place as shall be designated in the writ before the supreme judicial court, or before some justice thereof, in term time or vacation, and whether the court is in session or not.[2]

[1] Pub. Sts. ch. 185, § 4.   [2] Ibid., § 5.

§ 241. In cases of imprisonment or restraint by a person not a sheriff, deputy sheriff or jailer, and it seems that the same form of writ may be used in any case, the writ shall be in the following form:

COMMONWEALTH OF MASSACHUSETTS.

[SEAL] To the Sheriffs of our several counties and to their respective deputies, *Greeting:*

We command you that the body of , of , by , of , imprisoned and restrained of his liberty, as it is said, you take and have before , a justice of our supreme judicial court at , immediately after the receipt of this writ, to do and receive what our said justice shall then and there consider concerning him in this behalf; and summon said then and there to appear before our said justice to show the cause of the taking and detaining of said ; and have you there this writ with your doings thereon.

Witness at , this day of , in the year .

The writ shall be signed by the justice of the peace issuing the same, and it may be served in any county by a sheriff or deputy sheriff thereof, or of any other county.[1]

§ 242. If the party is detained for a cause or offence for which he is bailable, he shall be admitted to bail if sufficient bail is offered ; and if not, he shall be remanded, with an order of the court or

[1] Pub. Sts. ch. 185. §§ 6, 7.

judge expressing the sum in which he shall be held
to bail, and the court at which he shall be required
to appear ; and any justice of the peace may, at any
time before the sitting of said court, bail the party
pursuant to such order.[1]

INSOLVENCY PROOFS.

§ 243. A justice of the peace may take proofs
in insolvency. The creditor in person, or if he is
unavoidably prevented from being present, his
agent, must make an oath before the justice of the
peace in substance as follows : —

I,　　　　, do swear that　　　　, of　　, by [or
against] whom proceedings in insolvency have been
instituted, at and before the date of such proceedings
was and still is justly and truly indebted to me in the
sum of　　, for which sum or any part thereof I have
not, nor has any other person to my use, to my knowledge or belief, received any security or satisfaction
whatever, beyond what has been disposed of agreeably
to law. And I do further swear that said claim was
not procured by me for the purpose of influencing the
proceedings in this case. And I do further swear that
I have not directly or indirectly made or entered into
any bargain, arrangement or agreement, express or
implied, to sell, transfer or dispose of my claim, or any
part of my claim, against said debtor, nor have directly
or indirectly received or taken, or made or entered into

any bargain, arrangement or agreement, express or implied, to take or receive, directly or indirectly, any money, property or consideration whatsoever to myself, or to any person or persons to my use or benefit, under or with any understanding or agreement, express or implied, whereby my vote for assignee or my assent to the debtor's discharge is or shall be in any way affected, influenced or controlled, or whereby the proceedings in this case are or shall be affected, influenced or controlled.[1]

INSPECTION OF DRUGGISTS' BOOKS AS TO LIQUOR SALES.

§ 244. Justices of the peace may inspect druggists' books, certificates and prescriptions of sales of intoxicating liquor.[2]

LIMITED PARTNERSHIP ACKNOWLEDGMENTS.

§ 245. A justice of the peace shall receive acknowledgments of limited partnership certificates. The certificate must be acknowledged by all the partners before the justice.[3]

MARRIAGES.

§ 246. A marriage may be solemnized by a justice of the peace who resides in the Commonwealth and continues to perform the functions of

---

[1] Pub. Sts. ch. 157, §§ 29–31.   [2] Sts. 1887, ch. 431, § 4.
[3] Pub. Sts. ch. 75, § 5.

his office; but every marriage shall be solemnized in the city or town in which the person solemnizing it resides, or in which one or both of the persons to be married reside.[1] Any form may be used by a justice of the peace in solemnizing a marriage.

§ 247. A justice of the peace shall receive a certificate of intention of marriage from the parties wishing to be married. This certificate is given to the parties by the clerk or registrar of the city or town where they respectively dwell, or in which they propose to have the marriage solemnized.[2]

§ 248. If the parties themselves make mutual agreements in the presence of a justice of the peace, with his assent, he undertaking to act in his official capacity, it is a legal marriage.[3]

§ 249. Every justice of the peace shall make a record of each marriage solemnized before him, and of all facts relating to the marriage which are required by law to be recorded. He shall also between the first and tenth days of each month return a copy of all such records for the month next preceding to the clerk or registrar of the city or town in which the marriage was solemnized, and shall, when one or both of the parties to the marriage resided in a city or town other than that in which the marriage was solemnized, return a copy of the record of such marriage to the clerk

---

[1] Pub. Sts. ch. 145, § 22.　　　[2] Ibid., §§ 16, 17.
[3] Milford v. Worcester, 7 Mass. 48.

or registrar of the city or town in which either party resided, and to the clerks or registrars of both cities or towns when the parties resided in different places. Every justice of the peace neglecting to make these returns shall forfeit for each neglect not less than twenty nor more than one hundred dollars.[1]

§ 250. A justice of the peace who joins persons in marriage contrary to the provisions above stated, knowing that the marriage is not duly authorized, shall forfeit not less than fifty nor more than one hundred dollars.[2]

§ 251. When a marriage appears to have been celebrated by a competent officer, as a justice of the peace, the marriage is deemed lawful, although it is not duly authorized by law, and although the justice of the peace may have incurred a penalty for his irregularity.[3]

§ 252. For lawfully certifying and solemnizing a marriage, a justice of the peace shall be entitled to receive one dollar and twenty-five cents.[4]

NOMINATIONS OF GUARDIANS.

§ 253. The nomination of a guardian by a minor above the age of fourteen years may be made before a justice of the peace, who shall certify the fact to the probate court.[5]

---

[1] Pub. Sts. ch. 145, § 24.
[2] Ibid., § 25.
[3] Milford v. Worcester, 7 Mass. 56.
[4] Pub. Sts. ch. 199, § 17.
[5] Ibid., ch. 139, § 3.

REMOVAL OF GATES, ETC., ON TOWN AND PRIVATE
WAYS.

§ 254. If fences, gates, rails or bars are upon
or across a town way or private way, they may be
removed by the order of a justice of the peace,
unless they are there placed for the purpose of
preventing the spreading of a disease dangerous to
the public health, or unless they are erected or
continued by license of the town, or of the person
for whose use such private way was laid out.[1]

§ 255. The power conferred upon justices of
the peace to order fences, gates, rails or bars across
town ways or private ways to be removed, is no
more a judicial power than if it had been vested
in the selectmen or in the surveyors of highways,
or than is the similar power which any citizen has,
to remove like obstructions in a county highway.
Thus not being a judicial power, an order of a
justice of the peace for the removal of such ob-
struction is not in the nature of a judicial warrant,
and the sheriff or his deputy is not required in his
official capacity to serve it [2]

WITNESSES.

§ 256. Every justice of the peace may issue
summonses for witnesses in all cases pending
before courts, magistrates, auditors, referees, arbi-

[1] Pub. Sts. ch. 54, § 5.   [2] Davis v. Smith, 130 Mass. 113.

trators and other persons authorized to examine witnesses; and the summons shall be in the form heretofore adopted and commonly used, but may be altered from time to time like other writs: provided however, that justices of the peace shall not issue summonses for witnesses in criminal cases unless requested so to do by the attorney-general or other person acting in the case in behalf of the state, or by the party prosecuted; and in the latter case, it shall be expressed in the summons that it is granted at the request of the party prosecuted; and the witness shall not be required to attend unless upon payment or tender of his legal fees.[1]

Form of Subpœna with duces tecum.

COMMONWEALTH OF MASSACHUSETTS.

S. } ss.

To A. B. of T., in the county of E., and within said
   Commonwealth.   *Greeting :*

You are hereby required, in the name of the Commonwealth of Massachusetts, to appear before the
court   , holden at   , within and for the
county of   , on the   day of   , at
      o'clock in the   noon, and from day to day
thereafter, until the action hereinafter named is heard
by said court, to give evidence of what you know relat-

---

[1] Sts. 1885, ch. 141, § 1.

ing to an action of   then and there to be heard
and tried between C. D. of M., in the county of S. and
within said Commonwealth, plaintiff, and E. F. of said
M.. defendant [if a simple subpœna without the *duces
tecum* is desired, the following may be omitted] ; [and
you are further required to bring with you [here state
what, if any, books, papers, etc., must be brought].]

Hereof fail not, as you will answer your default under
the pains and penalties in the law in that behalf made
and provided.

Dated at B. the   day of   , A. D. 189 .

S. P.,
Justice of the Peace.

§ 257. The fees of justices of the peace for a
subpœna for one or more witnesses shall be ten
cents.[1]

[1] Pub. Sts. ch. 199, § 1.

INDEX.

INDEX.

www.ingramcontent.com/pod-product-compliance
Lightning Source LLC
Chambersburg PA
CBHW020543270326
41927CB00006B/702